Dr. Hall's memoir is a story of hope, growth, and perseverance, and I applaud her for being so candid. Dr. Kellye Hall's name is one our young ladies of all ages should be familiar with. Her memoir evokes all emotions, and after reading it twice, symbolically, I am standing up and giving her a standing ovation. This is a book our young Black girls need in their collection to show that with God and willpower, dreams can be accomplished. This book deserves a spot right next to Michelle Obama's book!

Kiera Vargas, JD, MLIS, MS

Dr. Kellye Worth Hall's memoir is a testament to the power of knowing oneself, learning one's blind spots, owning one's opportunities for growth, and staying true to one's race to achieve personal and professional goals. In Kellye's memoir, she tells us how she got across the finish line. We'll have to read her second memoir to learn what happens AFTER crossing the finish line!

Dr. Chandra Sledge Mathias, Ed.D

I really like how Dr. Kellye Worth Hall set the groundwork early on in her book regarding her faith in Jesus Christ. People can understand that her Source of Strength has propelled her to do great things and how the reader too can put their faith in Him while on their personal journey. This book is also funny and animated in ways that balance some of the seriousness.

Trent Thomas, LPN

I love this book. *I am the Beat, God sets the Pace* is a must-read. Dr. Kellye W. Hall shares some very thought-provoking stories about her life. She shares with readers the good, the bad, and the ugly parts of her life. Dr. Hall takes readers on a creative journey using unique song titles to express her life throughout the book. Most of all, she ties scriptures to each chapter to encourage readers to use their faith to navigate through tough times.

Dr. Ashley Little
CEO/Founder Ashley Little Enterprises, LLC,
13x bestselling author

Holy Bible, New International Version®, NIV® Copyright ©1973, 1978, 1984, 2011 by Biblica, Inc.® Used by permission. All rights reserved worldwide.
NIV Reverse Interlinear Bible: English to Hebrew and English to Greek. Copyright © 2019 by Zondervan.

Holy Bible, King James Version, KJV is public domain in the United States.

Holy Bible, New Living Translation, copyright © 1996, 2004, 2015 by Tyndale House Foundation. Used by permission of Tyndale House Publishers, Inc., Carol Stream, Illinois 60188. All rights reserved.

Scripture taken from the New King James Version®. Copyright © 1982 by Thomas Nelson. Used by permission. All rights reserved.

Good News Translation (GNT)
Copyright © 1992 by American Bible Society

Amplified Bible (AMP)
Copyright © 2015 by The Lockman Foundation, La Habra, CA 90631. All rights reserved.

ISBN: 978-1-952840-08-1

UNITED HOUSE Publishing
Waterford, Michigan
info@unitedhousepublishing.com
www.unitedhousepublishing.com

Cover and interior design: Matt Russell, Marketing Image, mrussell@marketing-image.com

Cover Illustration by: Todgi Dozier of The Black Onion www.theblackonion.com

Author Photo: Krista Jasso https://kristajasso.myportfolio.com/work
                Darrell Alston linktr.ee/shotbyinvisiond

Printed in the United States of America
2021—First Edition

SPECIAL SALES
Most UNITED HOUSE books are available at special quantity discounts when purchased in bulk by corporations, organizations, and special-interest groups. For information, please e-mail orders@ unitedhousepublishing.com.

To Kedeja, all the young ladies I have mentored,
and all those I will mentor. You've inspired me
more than you'll ever know.

TABLE OF CONTENTS

I WAS HERE

I never really thought my life was that interesting until I started telling people about it. People have told me I've done amazing things. Over the years, I never intended to do anything amazing. I was just doing what I thought would be fun or what God created me to do. Once I realized many people like me weren't doing some of the things I was doing, I then began to see I was unique.

The journey of writing a book has been a long one. I started on one path, but God made it clear I was to take another. What began as something to do other than medicine, became a story someone needs to read. This story, my story, is told the only way I know how: with brutal honesty. People think they know me, but they only know what I allow them to see. This memoir is a small glimpse into who I really am and how I came to be Kellye Nichelle Worth Hall, M.D.

I want to inspire people, yet I want to entertain as well. This is why I created Nickye Storm, my alter ego. There are many different sides to me, and I often feel they conflict with each other-I can be fun and outgoing, yet, I can also be moody and introverted. Kellye is who I consider the wholesome, lovable, re-served me. Nickye is the loud, in your face, confident, sometimes arrogant, me, who typically just resides in my head or my performance personality. The idea to put Nickye in the book came from a series of books I read by E L James. She wrote with her subconscious as a character, and I really liked the idea for my book because, oftentimes, what I present to the world is a much kinder version of what I really want to say or do. My editors liked her, so I kept her in. Nickye would get me in trouble if she spoke because she has no filter, so I try my best to censor her most times.

I have also integrated my love of music into the book. The chapter titles are actually song titles from some of my favorite songs or artists. Whatever I do, I try to stay true to myself, and I want people to get a glimpse of all my parts. This is just the beginning of books to come. I'm not good at making up stories, so while some of this book may seem like it never really happened, it did. Some details are clearer than others, and some of the spoken words I wrote from other people are not verbatim. But for the most part, when I am speaking, what I put in quotation marks was actually what came out of my mouth. Someone that was mentoring me early on as I was writing this book, once implied they weren't convinced I was as bold as I was, as young as I was. They didn't believe some of the things I said. But they clearly didn't know me. You might think I tell my story so well, I must have made it up. I didn't. This is my real life, and this is who I am. To keep from getting myself into too much trouble, I did change the names of several people. However, I did keep the actual names of people that gave me permission to do so.

My book is going to speak more sincerely to a specific group of people, but I feel like there are little take-home nuggets for those in various walks of life. Because I thrive on mentoring and encouraging others, I have added little exercises for you, the reader, as a way to draw you to the Word of God and prayerfully motivate you to become a better version of yourself. I am not a Bible scholar and my interpretations of the scriptures are affected by my personal experiences and gleanings. I am not Ms. Sally Super Saint, but I've lived some life, and I want to help others learn from what I've done right and from what I've done wrong. Some scriptures actually helped me to get through tough times, and others are more recent revelations that have come with my maturation in Christ. Most importantly, I feel called to share my faith with you to help you make it through tough times. If you've ever felt like you were at a disadvantage because you are either a woman, black, underrepresented, misunderstood, economically at a disadvantage, or for one reason or another, you just didn't fit in; if you are a combination of two or more of the previously stated, this book is for you. I want you to know that despite obstacles, you can achieve whatever you believe, and if you follow God's promptings, He will help you to succeed. *BARS* With that, allow me to reintroduce myself.

Finally, be strong in the Lord and in his mighty power.
Put on the full armor of God, so that you can take your
stand against the devil's schemes. For our struggle is not against
flesh and blood, but against the rulers, against the authorities,
against the powers of this dark world and against the spiritual
forces of evil in the heavenly realms. Therefore put on the full
armor of God, so that when the day of evil comes, you may be
able to stand your ground, and after you have done everything,
to stand. Stand firm then, with the belt of truth buckled around
your waist, with the breastplate of righteousness in place,
and with your feet fitted with the readiness that comes from
the gospel of peace. In addition to all this, take up the shield
of faith, with which you can extinguish all the flaming arrows
of the evil one. Take the helmet of salvation and the sword
of the Spirit, which is the word of God.

Ephesians 6:10-17, NIV

CHAPTER ONE

Brenda's Got a Baby

You have heard me teach things that have been confirmed by many reliable witnesses. Now teach these truths to other trustworthy people who will be able to pass them on to others.

2 Timothy 2:2, NLT

Many people believe they are victims of their environment or circumstances. It took years for me to learn this isn't necessarily true and doesn't always have to be the case. Fortunately, my parents made me believe I could do anything I set my mind to; I didn't have to accept mediocrity. I wish more people had the same experience.

I witnessed the power of encouragement in the case of two young ladies I encountered while working in the emergency department (ED). These two ladies had similar lifestyles and upbringings, but their outcomes were polar opposites. I'll start with the young lady with whom I had the least contact. She was a young black female, eighteen to be exact. She lived in the "hood" in Charlotte, and she came to the ED because she was having abdominal pain. The first thing we do when females over the age of ten come in with abdominal pain is order a pregnancy test. Unbeknownst to her, she was pregnant. As I looked at her results, prior to entering the room, I imagined I would be telling this patient she was pregnant, and then she would be devastated.

I walked into the room to find her with her mother. If I had to take a guess, I would say the mother was about the same age I was, which was thirty-five at the time. I was dreading the conversation even more because I felt like I was going to have to deal with two disappointed people now, not just the patient. I pulled my doctor's stool out from under the sink, wheels squeaking as I rolled it along the floor. I took a seat next to the stretcher the patient was so nonchalantly lying on. Before I delivered the news, I stated, "Hello, I'm Dr. Hall. Who do you have here with you?"

She said, "This my mom."

"Is it okay if we discuss your results with her in the room?" She was not a minor, which meant I didn't have to speak about any medical information with her parent. Therefore, I wanted to give her the opportunity to have Mom step out if she wanted.

She answered, "It's all good."

"Well, I understand you came in for abdominal pain." I paused before delivering the news, wondering if I should get more history. I figured there was no reason to belabor the point. "So, your pregnancy test came back positive," I announced.

The reaction I had been expecting was not the reaction I got. Instead of tears and doubts about the future, she looked at me wide-eyed and smiled. "I'm pregnant?" she said with glee. I was confused. I began to think about how I would react if I'd found out I was pregnant at that age. No smile would have been on my face. I thought about how my mom would have reacted and the angry scowl she would have given me. I had goals at that age, and a pregnancy would have significantly hindered those plans.

There was Nickye in that emergency room. She stood with arms folded and smacked her lips while nodding her head in disapproval. I stopped daydreaming and turned and faced the mom. Shockingly, she responded, "Well it's about time!" I was just dumbfounded. Nickye raised her hand, ready to slap some sense into Mom. I looked at the two of them in disbelief and then quickly fixed my face as I came to the reality I was the physician in the scenario. I went on to finish the encounter, and when I walked out of the room to go back to the doctors' charting station, I allowed the fakeness to come off my face. Since I wasn't facing the patient and her mom, I could react the way I wanted. What did her mom mean? *It's about time?* Was she hoping for her teenager to have a child? Why wasn't she upset like I was?

I just started being nosy at that point. Please don't judge me. God was and is still working on me. I looked through her chart and saw where she lived and that she had no insurance. I was angry because I figured she was another black female who was going to become one of the statistics I hate: a single, black, teenage parent living off the system. As a black woman, it disturbs me when people don't have dreams and aspirations beyond their current situation. Sometimes I find myself wishing people would just try in life, even though it's clearly not my business. This brings me to the second young lady.

In some medical facilities, scribes do the charting for the practitioners.

Scribes are typically college students, and many of them take the job because they are interested in pursuing a career in the medical field. In the emergency department, I ran into a variety of scribes, but there was one in particular who I felt I could relate to on a more personal level. Her name was Kedeja. She was a nineteen-year-old black female going to school at a local community college. She had her hair in long braids at the time, and she kind of reminded me of myself when I was in college. During some downtime one day, I asked, "So, what are you trying to do with your life?"

Because we had not worked together or interacted much prior to this, I guess she was surprised I was interested. She responded, "I'm thinking about going to PA school."

"Why PA school and not medical school?" I asked.

She looked perplexed as if the thought had never crossed her mind. "I don't know."

Instantly, I went into mentor mode. "The reason I ask is because PAs do the exact same thing as a doctor, but they get paid half as much. So, I say, get paid what you're worth."

I could see she was pondering what to say next, so I interrupted her thoughts. "Just think about it."

Kedeja and I would only work together here and there because physicians never got the same scribe all the time. Our shifts varied. But I felt comfortable around her. Because of that, I would share my life experiences with her, and I talked about how much fun I had at North Carolina Agricultural and Technical State University, otherwise known as A&T, where I earned my undergraduate degree. I hadn't worked with her for a couple of months when we had our next shift together. Before we started work for the day, she looked at me in amazement and said, "Dr. Hall, I don't know what you said to me, but I took a tour of A&T, and I liked it. So, I applied and got accepted, and I'll be transferring there in the fall."

My mouth dropped so wide that she could probably see my tonsils. I shook my head in disbelief and I exclaimed, "What?"

She laughed and nodded her head.

"No; you didn't!"

She continued, gesturing "yes," while I began to feel like I had just made a difference in the world. "But I wasn't even trying to get you to go to A&T. I was just doing what I do best, which is talk people's heads off."

She laughed. "Well whatever you did, it worked."

From that day forth, I began officially mentoring her, even when she went away to college, and that's when I discovered she wasn't so different from the eighteen-year-old patient who was happy she was pregnant.

They were about the same age when I met them and grew up in similar neighborhoods just miles from each other. When Kedeja and I started working together, I didn't know anything about how she grew up. But over time and numerous lunches we spent together, she told me she was born and raised in the "hood" of Charlotte. Three years into our relationship, she confided she lived with her dad and had started working in high school to take care of him because he became ill. At one of our mentoring lunches, she poured out her life story to me.

"I flunked the ninth grade."

I almost choked on my pink lemonade. "You did what, now?"

She shrugged her shoulders, "I wasn't motivated. My dad would wake me up and ask me if I was going to school. I would get up, put on clothes, sit on the porch, and watch my bus go down the street, and I wouldn't get on it."

"Kedeja, no way!"

"I was horrible in the beginning of high school. I wasn't motivated, I didn't study, and I have a bunch of tattoos." She then began pointing out the decorative artwork on her brown skin.

As she was saying this to me, I looked on incredulously. She continued with her confession.

"I remember being alone in my house one day when I was supposed to be at school and suddenly thinking, *I'm not supposed to be here*. I would tell my family, and they would be like, "Yeah, whatever." They didn't believe me. That's when I turned things around and started getting serious about school. I skipped a grade, so I still ended up graduating on time. I'm the first in my family to go to college."

I couldn't believe it. That was not the Kedeja I thought I knew. My curiosity was aroused. I asked, "Before meeting me and the other black doctors you worked with, had you ever seen a black doctor before?"

"No," she replied. "Then, when I started talking to you and Dr. Phillips, I realized maybe I could be a doctor too. Y'all changed my life."

Her saying those words actually changed *my* life. I grew up never thinking I would fail, never expecting to be less than successful, while she grew up pretty much the opposite. She had no clue of her potential. When I spoke positivity into her life, it changed her future, and that wasn't even my intention. Kedeja excelled at A&T and is now thriving in medical school. When I think back to the pregnant eighteen-year-old, I wonder if someone like me speaking different expectations into her life could have made a difference. Unfortunately, I don't know her on a personal level, and likely will not come across her again, but it doesn't mean I can't try to put other young people like her on a course to personal achievement.

MOMENT OF REFLECTION

Has there been someone that made a positive impact on your life? If you are able, take time to thank the person or people who molded you. If you are unable to speak to them directly, take the time to send them a letter or some sort of message. Is there someone in your life that you could be an example to? Foster a relationship where you can share your life experience with someone who wants to walk in your shoes. Mentoring doesn't have to take a lot of time or effort. Sometimes, all you need to do is discuss how you got to where you are, and you can change someone's life for the better.

18

CHAPTER TWO

Isn't She Lovely

But others fell into good ground, and brought forth fruit,
some an hundredfold, some sixtyfold, some thirtyfold.
Who hath ears to hear, let him hear.

Matthew 13:8-9, KJV

I was born on June 5th, 1978 in Rochester, New York. I came out of the womb with blonde hair and blue eyes. People thought I was white. My dad's running joke is that when he saw me, he playfully shouted, "Who y'all got over there on that table?" As if they had replaced my mom with a white woman. I would say I get my charm and wit from my dad; although I always felt like that joke was corny, maybe because I heard it a million times. Apparently, the hospital tried to put caucasian on my birth certificate. My dad didn't think that was a joke. He expeditiously corrected that mistake. Well, that's all I can say about New York. My parents moved to North Carolina when I was ten months old, so I don't know Rochester. I saw a picture of cars covered with snow where we lived, and that's the end of my Rochester story and memories.

My dad is from Raleigh, North Carolina, and my mom is from Ft. Lauderdale, Florida. They met in college, at A&T. My dad got a job in real estate trying to sell off properties in what was supposed to be a thriving town run by black people called Soul City, North Carolina. The county I grew up in had a lot of important people living in it. I didn't appreciate the influential people with whom my dad was involved until I was older.

For instance, Soul City was the brainchild of Floyd McKissick, a civil rights attorney, born in Asheville, North Carolina. When we lived in Soul City, I remember visiting his house occasionally. I knew him as Uncle Floyd when I was little, but I would later discover he was my dad's mentor. I didn't have many interactions with Uncle Floyd because he was constantly busy, but when in a room with him, one just knew he was powerful. He commanded attention, and it impressed me, even at an early age, how people acted around him. As an adult, I found out that he was one of the first black students at the University of North Carolina at Chapel Hill's law school. He actually had a three-year legal battle before he was allowed to enroll. He had even more battles once he was a student there, but that's a different story. I don't even remember him being the founder of Soul City when I was little. Much of that revelation came after I began to understand the whole Civil Rights Movement. You would think I would have been taught information like that in my school, seeing how the county was predominantly black. However, at that time, white people were more influential in the county. White people being more influential despite being less in number is a recurring theme that has remained true today. Black history is often kept out of American history because our history is regularly erased. My dad became the first black county manager in Warren County, where I grew up. That was not taught in our history classes either. I believe my drive to be successful also came from my dad. Of course, my mom played a role as well, but seeing all the battles my dad had to fight because he was a black male made me a fighter too.

Getting back to Soul City: It was built in the heart of Ku Klux Klan country and on the lands of an antebellum plantation. Mr. McKissick had big dreams. He envisioned the lands that were once worked by slaves would be run by a black man and inhabited by both black and white residents living equal lives. However, his vision got shut down by Senator Jesse Helms. The senator prevented Soul City from getting government funding by accusing McKissick of mishandling the money. Therefore, the city is more of a township and is pretty much just residential. The original plan was to have shops and a factory to bring jobs to the area. The factory got built, but later, everything came to a halt, and the factory that was once there became a prison. Imagine that, a prison replacing a job-market in a predominantly black neighborhood.

Someone else I grew up around but didn't realize was so influential until later, was Jane Ball-Groom. She was part of the Soul City development team and has actually written a memoir about Soul City titled *The Salad Pickers: Journey South.* She is the mother of one of my former babysitters and was one of many mothers I had in the community. She lived in the next circle over from the one in which I grew up. She was there from the beginning. A transplant from New York, she uprooted her family to promote the dream of a city owned by a black man. Despite the fact the Soul City New Town Project never developed into the flourishing community it was supposed to be, she is still there helping to keep the dream alive so the community can be revitalized. I always found her to be such a wealth of knowledge, and I loved going to her house because she was so warm and inviting. She was the kind of person that made someone feel important with her gentle tone and infectious laugh. But because she was a northerner, one could also tell that if you rubbed her the wrong way, you would regret it.

Soul City was a great place to grow up in the '80s and '90s. It was made up of a group of streets that ended in little cul-de-sacs. The individual circles formed one large circle that made up the residential part. In my circle, there were a bunch of girls of various ages who resided in a few of the houses and some older guys in another house. The parents of another former babysitter of mine were also part of the inception of Soul City. Her dad was a developer for the town, and her mom worked as director of the cultural arts program. I just knew them as surrogate parents. Because her dad was in the same fraternity as my dad and her mom was in the same sorority as my mom, we were at many events and gatherings together. If we ever needed something, they were more than happy to oblige. However, all of the parents in our circle were friends, and all of the kids were that way too. We spent our free time either going to the basketball court down the street, riding bicycles, or dancing to music in our own circle. Everyone looked out for each other, and everyone who lived in Soul City knew each other. That sense of community was another of the reasons I was able to succeed in my early life.

There's a saying, "It takes a village to raise a child." Well, in Soul City, that was true. Families helped each other out. Many of the families in Soul City were middle class, with similar values. A sense of black pride and upward mobility were goals of many, and this was passed along from house to house. If a neighboring adult caught a kid attempting to do wrong, it was reported to the child's parent immediately. Higher education was usually spoken about as a normal expectation, and kids were frequently part of groups that stressed the importance of learning. Because many of the leaders in the community were respected for the strides they made, not only in the community of Soul City but in the black community in general, we were taught to desire more and not stand for less.

What I didn't realize was Soul City and Warren County were considered under-served areas. Despite the homes and the residents of Soul City consisting of middle-class families, Warren County was considered to be an area of poverty. The funny thing is because I and many of my friends didn't live in poverty, I never knew others around me did. I didn't know my school was under-funded because who knows these things as a child, especially living in a rural area? Many of the neighboring schools appeared similar, so I never felt like

I was missing out on anything. Perspective as a child is interesting. You believe what you're told. Because I was applauded and congratulated for academic success, I was put in programs to help me succeed even further. I was oblivious to anything outside my own world. While I and many of my close friends have gone on to live prosperous and fruitful lives, a lot of my classmates are living in Warren County earning menial wages. The drastic variation in the lives and careers of my classmates is a prime example that it is possible to overcome your upbringing by being exposed to things outside your community.

My parents both had undergraduate degrees and master's degrees, and because my dad is a member of Omega Psi Phi Fraternity Inc., and my mom is a member of Delta Sigma Theta Sorority Inc., my friends and I went on college tours, and my family visited different areas of the country. Members of these organizations were professionals in various fields, and because I was reared around doctors, dentists, lawyers, educators, and other middle-class people, I never knew that theoretically, I was less likely to succeed because of where I grew up.

After resigning as County Manager, my dad got a position as the district manager for Congresswoman Eva Clayton, also a resident of Warren County. She was a woman who got things done. She was always fighting against injustice, and I admired her greatly. As a teen, my family would go to cookouts at her lake house and ride her boat. Her son even let me drive the boat a few times. If it had not been for the people who were in my life in the early years, maybe I wouldn't have believed anything was possible for me. What I hope you realize is this: a significant number of black people grow up in undesirable locations and have a plethora of things they have to overcome, but when they are exposed to something better and believe they can achieve, they can prevail over the obstacles that keep so many down. At that time, as I was growing up, I didn't think I had anything to overcome, but the fact of the matter is, I did. Society makes it seem like growing up in a predominantly black neighborhood and going to predominantly black schools automatically puts you at a disadvantage. While I may not have had some of the bells and whistles of a better-funded school, my parents made sure to find opportunities outside school, where I could learn more.

I am grateful God placed such amazing and inspiring people in my life because I had a number of people I could look to as sources of inspiration for future success. There weren't necessarily specific things these people said to me, but it was the excellence they exuded. Kids are often influenced by what they see. So, when I saw people that had the respect of others in the community, I wanted to be like them. They were people of action, and they created their own lanes. I was a kid who wanted to be a leader and not a follower. I wanted people to admire me like I admired those adults I grew up around. Failure was never an option for me because those who influenced me always seemed to win. When all I witnessed was success, that's all I saw for my future.

MOMENT OF REFLECTION

Are you on good ground? Meaning, when people speak wisdom or instruction in your life, are you receptive? Think back over your life and reflect on the decisions you made. Were some of those decisions influenced by others? What was it they said that motivated you? Do you speak good into others? Think about people in your life now and make a conscious effort to impart words of wisdom to someone who could use it.

CHAPTER THREE

Darling Nikki

*The one who guards his mouth [thinking before he speaks]
protects his life; The one who opens his lips wide
[and chatters without thinking] comes to ruin.*

Proverbs 13:3, AMP

Let me give a little more background on the differences between Kellye and my alter ego Nickye Storm. As I alluded to before, Nickye is my wise-aleck side that is sort of a bad girl and also my performance personality. She's the person inside that I sometimes have to keep inward. There are various situations in which I'm thinking one thing, but because it would be inappropriate or rude, Kellye cleans it up to a more presentable statement or reaction. I don't actually have multiple personalities, but I would say that, depending on what the situation calls for, one can see a difference in how I act. For example, I can be a professional and interact with CEOs, but I can easily bring out my playful side and make teenagers feel I can relate to them. While I might be serious on one hand, I can be silly on the other. I know which personality to bring out at the right time.

For the most part, Kellye is who I really am, but I like to say Nickye Storm is like Beyoncé's Sasha Fierce. Sometimes I can be reserved and quiet, but if someone upsets me, or if I'm doing some sort of performing, Nickye steps in, so I thought it would be fun to incorporate her in my story.

I would say Nickye really came to life when I was in high school, but I've always been feisty, so touches of Nickye were apparent in my earlier life too. For instance, when I was a young child, if my family was preparing to go somewhere, my mom would have the duty of getting me and my sisters dressed. My dad typically wouldn't help much, maybe not because he didn't want to, but probably because he didn't really get how to adequately dress and do the hair of three girls. One time, when there was just my sister Kim and me, before our baby sister Kourtnye was born, my mom was frantically trying to get herself, Kim, and me ready, and my dad sat in anguish because he knew we would be late.

Dad said, "Laurie, we have to go!"

"Charles, I'm moving as fast as I can," replied Mom.

Here I go, being disrespectful, but honest: "Well, Daddy, if you would help, maybe she could move faster."

I couldn't have been more than five or six at the time. I would have to say my pop-off attitude came from my mom and her side of the family. They were and still are no-nonsense and not afraid to tell you what they really think.

In elementary school, I was often shy, which people can't believe because I appear so outgoing today. But I was. I would sit under my mom and would be reluctant to play with other kids if I didn't know them. I came out of my shell when I started performing in talent shows in sixth grade. I really started growing into a performer by eighth grade, and I gained more and more confidence by the time I reached high school. By eleventh grade, I was more vocal and less fearful. I loved to show off and prove people wrong. While I was respectful, I was determined to make a mockery of people if they didn't believe I could do something.

When I was a senior in high school, I was involved in some of everything. I was a drum major for the marching band and soloist in the concert band. I also ran track, played basketball, and then changed clothes to cheer for the boys. I did all of this while maintaining my grades to be on the honor roll.

I recall an incident when I completely fooled someone because he misread my cover and thought I was one type of book when I really was another. We didn't make it to the playoffs in girls' basketball, but the boys made it that year, and since I was a cheerleader, I got to go along to root for our boys. We were the away team, and while the team was going through shoot-around before the game, my cheerleading squad was stretching and getting ready along the sidelines. A basketball rolled my way, and as I picked it up close to the three-point line, the other school's principal yelled over to me:

"If you shoot a shot from there, I'll buy you whatever you want from the concession stand."

Nickye glared at him while she egged me on to show him who was boss. I abruptly switched out of my perky cheerleader act and switched over to my tomboyish stance. I smirked at the principal with his chauvinistic smile, dribbled the ball a couple of times, and shot the ball with perfect arc while leaving my right hand up awaiting the swish. All net! Once it went in, I turned to see the shock on the principal's face and sarcastically curtsied, lifting my cute cheerleading skirt.

"What you didn't know was I play shooting guard for the girls' team," I smirked.

Once the principal realized he got played, he smiled and shook my hand. "A deal is a deal. Let's go."

Nickye was already at the concession stand ordering food.

I thrived off situations like that, and as I've matured, my resolve to debunk anyone's false theories has grown exponentially. While I can present myself in an appropriate fashion, my inner thoughts can often be cynical and ornery. On the other hand, while I loved performing, I could get slightly nervous, therefore, the need for Nickye would arise. Giving myself an alter-ego allows me to show out in a way I sometimes don't feel I could as Kellye. Kellye and Nickye are true representations of me as a Gemini, known for having opposing personalities in one body. Kellye is the good twin, while Nickye is the sometimes not-so-good twin.

MOMENT OF REFLECTION

How are you at holding your tongue? Have there been times you said something you wished you could take back? Think of an instance when you said the wrong thing, and consider the repercussions of your words. Now, give thought to a time when you wanted to say something that was negative, but you were able to control yourself. How did that situation end? Ponder the two scenarios, and meditate on how harmful/beneficial your actions were.

CHAPTER FOUR

Eye of the Tiger

But as for you, be strong and do not lose courage,
for there is reward for your work.

2 Chronicles 15:7, AMP

When I was in medical school, my mom saw my kindergarten teacher, Ms. Norwood, in the grocery store. Ms. Norwood was memorable. She was a nice teacher, but she gave me my first painful punishment in elementary school. I was talking when I wasn't supposed to, and as my punishment, Ms. Norwood popped me on the hand with a thick paddle she had fashioned by taping five rulers together. Whack! My hand stung like a jellyfish had just attacked me. The pain wasn't what made me shut up and act right. I didn't like thinking that Ms. Norwood was mad at me. To this day, I don't like to disappoint people. I typically didn't get in trouble for that very reason. I was always aiming to please and trying to overachieve.

When Ms. Norwood saw my mom in the store, she asked, "So what's Kellye doing?"

My mom proudly answered, "She's in medical school."

Ms. Norwood wasn't surprised. "I always knew that child was going to do something special. When all the other kids were playing with baby dolls, she was telling another student she was going to deliver a baby."

What did I know about delivering a baby at the age of five? As I said, it had to be God-ordained. I was listening to God before I knew it was God talking to me. What I mean is, I was always putting myself in a position to be the best because I felt like it was what I was supposed to do.

This desire to excel was best displayed through sports in my primary school life. Back in my day, we didn't have competitive recreational sports in our rural setting. Today, kids start participating in sports almost as soon as they learn to run. I didn't really have the opportunity to get involved in competitive sports until I got to middle school. I played volleyball in the fall, basketball in the winter, and softball in the spring. I tried to do it all. I felt I needed a surplus of things to do, otherwise, I would get bored and not be able to focus on anything. As I reflect on my life now, I think I probably had a small element of Attention Deficit Disorder, but because I was highly functioning, nobody ever knew that I had difficulty focusing.

Someone inspired me at an early age though-Mary Parker Coleman. She was amazing! She was white and born without a right hand. She was in eighth grade when I was in seventh grade. She played shooting guard during basketball season and pitcher during softball season. This chick could ball. She didn't let her lack of two fully formed limbs stop her. She was better than all of us. She could shoot three-pointers, and she was a natural-born leader. In softball, when she pitched, she had her glove resting on the edge of her arm where her hand would have been, and when she released the ball, she would quickly flip her glove on her opposite hand so she would be prepared to catch if the ball came her way. Watching her maneuver so gracefully was inspiring in itself. She never seemed to fret about being born with only one hand, and because she was such a great athlete, I never saw anyone pick on her. I studied her, and in my mind, I thought, if she can succeed with her deformity as an obstacle, I have no excuse but to succeed. She made me want to do better.

In seventh grade, I tried outfield for softball. That was a no-go because I was terrible. I couldn't judge where the ball would land, so I typically missed it. When a ball was hit high in the air toward the outfield, I would hear the crack of the bat, and I would instantly get nervous when I saw the ball coming in my direction. I would run forward, thinking it was going to land in front of me, only to run too far infield and see the ball travel over my head and bounce past me. It was quite embarrassing, actually. I tried short-stop, and I was better at that position, but I wasn't good enough to start in seventh grade. Because I'm an overachiever, I was determined I would be a better player the next year. Here's where God comes in, though, at that time, I didn't know it was God.

There were too many people who were better than me in basketball, so I knew I wasn't going to be the key player on the team. Early on, I learned my strengths, and I knew where to focus the most time so I could be the most effective and productive. As a result, I didn't try really hard to be the star in basketball. Still, since I liked the sport and needed to always be involved in something, I continued to play. I figured I had a chance to be the focal point of the softball team though if I could learn to pitch. Mary Parker Coleman was going to high school, and we didn't have anybody that was in line to fill her place. That's when I felt a prompting to fill the void that would be left.

The summer prior to my eighth-grade year, I focused all of my energy on learning to pitch. Nobody showed me; I watched Mary Parker Coleman. I would make my younger sister Kim practice with me as my catcher more days than not that summer. She had no interest in softball. One day, she threw down her glove and said, "I don't want to do this." She then stomped into the house leaving me to come up with plan B. Instead of having a person to throw to, I had to throw at a target I imagined on the side of the house.

At that point, I could have stopped, but I kept on training because I just knew that was what I was supposed to do. I actually spoke to myself before I threw the ball saying things like, "You're going to throw this perfectly over the plate," or "Keep your eye on the target. You can do it." That's where I would say I started learning to meditate. At the time, I didn't realize talking to myself was very elementary prayer, and God was actually listening. No one ever showed me or coached me on how to accurately pitch a softball, but I had great form for someone self-taught. Natural talent like that has to come from God's favor.

When softball season came around, I'm pretty sure Mr. Shulenburger, our coach, was trying to figure out who he was going to get to pitch. He had a couple of girls that started in other positions the prior year in mind. He'd planned to try to convert them to pitchers, but he gave anyone a chance who wanted it. There were about three of us who attempted pitching. I'll never forget his long, lanky legs as he walked by each of us, closely assessing our form, while we were all in a line pitching. I was last in the line, and as I threw, he looked astonished, and he said with his country twang, "Keep working on it, gal." That was enough motivation for me.

In the end, I was rewarded with the pitching position, and I was pretty good. Our team was mediocre, and we lost more than we won, but it didn't matter to me because, at the end of the season, I won MVP. Plus, I enjoyed the sport. I went from riding the bench to starting and winning MVP all in one year. I was proud I taught myself to pitch.

I did the same thing when I got to high school. Mary Parker Coleman was there, and I knew I wasn't going to be starting in softball over her, so I didn't even try to be an overachiever as a freshman. I joined the marching band since I knew I wanted to be in the marching band in college. The fall was dedicated specifically to marching band. I played basketball once the marching band season was over but was once again average. I didn't play anything in the spring of my freshman year.

In my sophomore year, I joined the track team, another seemingly random prompting by God. I ran the 100-meter dash and was put on the 4x100 meter relay team as a result. Mary Parker Coleman ran track in the beginning because she wasn't going to be starting in softball either. She was one of my teammates on the 4x100 team. My relay team won All-Conference two of the three years I was on the team. Our team made it to the state track meet all three years. Crystal Cooper was the girl at my school to beat in track most years. We were friends because we were in academically gifted (AG) classes together, but I was always a competitor, so I wanted to be as fast as her. She was the Mary Parker Coleman of track. She was another of my 4x100 teammates. She also ran the 100 meters, and I could never beat her—until senior year. Crystal was the anchor leg in the 4x100 meter relay the prior two years because she was the fastest, but I got faster, and by senior year, I was the anchor leg. That felt like a major accomplishment to me because I started beating Crystal at the 100 meters as well.

Once again, I felt a prompting, and before, I never had any interest in running hurdles, but something, or someone, prompted me to learn. Our track coach was a big guy, so he wasn't able to physically teach me any form, but he encouraged me to look at professional hurdlers like Florence Griffith-Joyner and Jackie Joyner-Kersee and imitate their styles. I was able to pick up on the fact the hurdlers only took three steps in between each hurdle before they jumped. Once I noticed that, I would practice until I only took three steps in between each hurdle. Junior year was when I started running the hurdles, and I was decent.

There was a girl, Awanya, from another school in our conference, who would win most of the time. I wanted to run hurdles like her. She won All-Conference in the 100-meter hurdles my junior year, but I was determined to beat her my senior year. I wasn't faster than some of the other girls in our conference, so I knew I wasn't going to be All-Conference in the 100 meters, but I figured maybe I could beat Awanya in the hurdles if I tried and be All-Conference in the hurdles.

In the Conference meet my senior year, I recall the 100-meter hurdles as if it happened yesterday. Awanya and I were in it of course, and we were in lanes adjacent to one another. She was the favorite to win, but I had beaten her in an earlier meet that year, so I was hopeful. We got lined up. The sun was beaming down on the track and although it was hot, I wasn't sweating.

"On your mark!"

I jumped up, stretched my legs, and tried to look intimidating like runners I'd watched on television. I imitated their steely gaze as I envisioned the finish line in the distance. I took my time, and then I crouched down into position.

"Get set!"

I lifted my buttocks up in the air and froze. I didn't want to risk a false start. I saw Awanya in my peripheral vision, and she seemed just as focused as me.

The starting gun fired: CRACK!

Awanya shot out in front of me. I wasn't the quickest off the blocks, but despite her having a head-start over me, I wasn't giving up. She was ahead of me for the first fifty meters, but either I picked up speed or she lost speed because suddenly, I was right beside her. I heard my dad in the background yelling, "Go, Kell, go!" I did go. I went right past Awanya in the last twenty-five meters, and I crossed the finish line first. Once again, I had set a goal, and I accomplished it. I'm pretty sure lengthening my stride to have a proper hurdler form is the reason I got faster and was able to beat Crystal my senior year.

That's how I became an overachiever. I always wanted to out-do the best. Unbeknownst to me, God was ordering my steps, and I obeyed. I carefully thought out where I had the chance to shine, and I worked my hardest at it. Despite starting out as average, I labored to make up for past failures, realizing situations and circumstances are not always going to be favorable, but determination can make the difference in success versus defeat.

MOMENT OF REFLECTION

How do you deal with life's struggles or obstacles? Do you let disappointments and defeats keep you down? Or do you look at these as opportunities to work harder and improve? Next time you want to give up because you weren't successful, think about the cost of giving up versus the cost of trying harder. Which option is more appealing to you and why? How often have you given up versus working harder? Think back over your life and determine if you are a fighter or if you are one to take an easier route.

CHAPTER FIVE

I Can

My feet have closely followed his steps;
I have kept to his way without turning aside.

Job 23:11, NIV

I was always a smart girl. Sometimes I think that was my downfall. I didn't have to try as hard as some other students to make good grades. Being naturally good at things could sometimes keep me from working hard. Instead, I just relied on my talents. Later in life, I discovered being naturally smart didn't make it easy to thrive in medical school. I figured out then I didn't know how to study efficiently, which eventually cost me.

I frequently won awards or received certificates for achievements in my early life. I was featured in the county newspaper a few times. The first time was in first grade because of a stitching I did of my favorite book at the time, *Charlotte's Web*. I won second place in a county-wide craft fair. Being reward-ed for doing good things early in my formative years made me crave success.

In the fourth grade, I won the spelling bee at my elementary school, which led me to the county-wide spelling bee. Despite loving attention, as I already stated, I started off a shy girl, so to do something like a spelling bee, in front of a couple of hundred people, was nerve-wracking. With every turn I took, walking to the microphone was a feat in itself. I spelled multiple words before my legs stopped feeling as limp as cooked spaghetti noodles. Everyone was so eerily quiet in the auditorium too. They were supposed to be, in order for contestants to concentrate, but it felt too silent. I could have heard an ant crawl across the floor as everyone waited for me to spell the words called out to me. We started out with thirty contestants and got down to the final four. As

I approached the front of the stage for my next word, I prepared myself.

"Nauseous," the pronouncer called out.

I froze. I didn't know what that word was. I looked at the pronouncer as if he'd suddenly started speaking another language. "Could you repeat the word please?" I asked

"Nauseous," the pronouncer repeated.

Well, that didn't work. The word was still foreign to me. What now? I was only one place away from making the regional spelling bee. I used the question all spelling bee participants use when they need more time to think.

"Could you use it in a sentence, please?"

"The medication made her nauseous."

I had never heard that word before, which was so ironic because the feeling in my stomach since I didn't know how to spell the word, was the exact word that I was given to spell. "Nauseous, N-O-S-H-O-U-S, nauseous." I hunched my shoulders because I had a gut feeling I was wrong.

I looked over at my parents and instantly knew my time was done. Fourth place was a good run and an accomplishment most people had not achieved, but I was so disappointed. My parents were proud of me, but I wasn't proud of myself. There was no chance I was going to the regional spelling bee unless one of the top three couldn't make it. I went home and cried in my pillow. I loathed the feeling of losing, which is likely why I strive so hard today. Interestingly enough, I didn't try out for the spelling bee again, even though I made it so far on my first attempt.

I kept working hard though, and it led me to be put in academically gifted classes. In high school, I had AG English, and the teacher, Mr. Lincoln, challenged our minds and beliefs, which was good, but it seemed like one day, he would be our best friend, and the next day, he was yelling hysterically at us for whispering in class. He made us read things like Homer's *The Iliad* and Chinua Achebe's *Things Fall Apart*. These are titles I would not typically have read on my own, but I appreciate him opening my eyes to these masterpieces. His class was one of the first classes to require more studying than typical, but luckily, I enjoyed reading, so I was receptive to the challenge.

My high school guidance counselor, Ms. Baker, thought she was doing me a favor when she suggested I apply to the University of North Carolina at Chapel Hill (UNC-CH). She was a nice older white woman, and she probably thought she was encouraging the smart little black girl to think bigger because she knew I wanted to be a doctor, and in her mind, she felt like my best opportunity to fulfill that goal was by going to UNC. I probably should have appreciated the fact she thought I was smart enough to go there, but because I was so pro-black at such an early age, I felt like she was saying my black school wasn't good enough to get me into medical school. She even asked my parents to have me consider applying somewhere else. Wrong answer. My dad wasn't hearing it either. At a parent-teacher conference, she spoke to my parents.

"Kellye is so gifted. She should really apply to UNC-Chapel Hill to give her the best chance in medical school."

My dad chuckled. "Nobody's stopping her. But if A&T was good enough for us, it's good enough for her too."

Ms. Baker looked astonished and appalled. She quickly straightened and changed the topic of conversation. Nickye was just beginning to blossom, but she waved her A&T flag right in Ms. Baker's face as she continued talking to my parents. My dad probably sparked Nickye's development. His resolve to be loud and braggadocious about doing life his way clearly influenced my rebellious nature at times.

Because I planned my life years in advance, I knew where I was going to college as a little girl. My parents went to A&T, and I loved A&T, including the band. That was where I was going. Since I knew that, I didn't apply to any other school because it wasn't like I was actually considering attending anywhere else. I would have been accepted into a myriad of places. Another of my dad's jokes, when people asked where I was going to go to college was, "She can go wherever she wants, but my money is going to A&T." This was fine with me because I developed a genuine love for the school. We had season tickets to the football games when I was in middle and high school, and prior to that, we never missed homecoming—ever. A few of my uncles went there, then my sisters and I all went, and then a cousin of mine went. Our love for the school is a family affair.

Here's the thing about A&T and probably Ms. Baker's concern. It's an HBCU. These are Historically Black Colleges and Universities. HBCUs are sometimes not respected as excellent institutions of higher learning as compared to predominantly white institutions, otherwise known as PWIs. Many of the schools have rich histories and prestigious alumni, however, they are highly underfunded and, therefore, overlooked by many students seeking to go to college. Because they are "black schools," graduates of these institutions can sometimes be viewed as less intelligent than those who went to PWIs. Typically that's not the case, but for so many, it's a false perception. A&T has always been a great school that has excelled in engineering, but it wasn't known for a great pre-medical program at the time. But, what I would later discover is, you don't need to have a pre-med major to get into medical school. As long as you took the required courses, you were able to apply to medical school regardless of your undergraduate institution.

There are a lot of reasons to go to HBCUs, but the main one is the experience. There's nothing like it. Campus life is something I can't really explain. It's like an inside joke you only understand if you went to an HBCU. The downside is a fair number of HBCUs are barely surviving because they're not supported enough by state funding. HBCUs have to fight for every dollar, and it's hard to compete with PWIs, especially since PWIs make so much money off black athletes, and their athletic departments can bring so much revenue and attention to their school. While A&T is now the number one HBCU in the nation, at the time, we were overshadowed by HBCUs like Howard University, Morehouse College, Spelman College, and Florida Agricultural and Mechanical University. By going to A&T in the late 90s, I was considered to be at a disadvantage when applying to medical school. But as have many other A&T alumni, I got into medical school just fine.

Being naturally smart, I didn't have to study as hard as other people. In later chapters, you'll see how that came to be a downfall for me. If I had studied more effectively, I might have had the chance to be number one in the class instead of number thirteen out of a little over a hundred students in my graduating class. However, I was able to obtain the Chancellor's scholarship at A&T, and I did it without an overwhelming amount of effort. I did my homework and paid attention in class, and for the most part, that was the extent of my studying. I did read chapters in books that were part of our assignments, but I didn't take much time breaking down and completely understanding the concepts. I memorized important things and did what I needed to do to get by.

Things did have to change a bit in college, and significantly so, by the time I made it to medical school. I didn't find anything easy about medical school, as I also reveal in future chapters. I almost wish I'd had to work a little harder earlier in life to achieve good grades. Maybe it would have kept me from having such a difficult time in medical school initially. I learned that forming good habits early on in life will help produce better outcomes later in life. Early in education, I only learned what I was interested in, so I didn't go above and beyond if it meant taking time away from something else I was more fascinated with. By the time I got to medical school, I realized I had a bit of a deficit in some foundational knowledge. In the beginning, that deficit made me question my intellect, but as always, failure was not an option, and I was just going to have to figure it out.

MOMENT OF REFLECTION

Think about a time someone tried to convince you to do what they thought was best for you, but you knew the path you should take. How did you react? Did you blindly heed their words or did you stay true to what you felt you should do? How did that make you feel? Did you make the right decision? Was it your own plan or God's? Immersing yourself in God's Word will help you to distinguish between God's plan for you versus your own plan.

CHAPTER SIX

Don't Stop the Music

*The Lord will keep you from all harm—he will watch over
your life; the Lord will watch over your coming
and going both now and forevermore.*
Psalm 121:7-8, NIV

Warren County was very rural, and there was hardly anything to do outside of school activities. My friends and I often went to Henderson, the next closest city. There wasn't a lot to do there either, but it was better than hanging out in "the Dub C," our nickname for Warren County. There was a teen club in Henderson we used to go to called The Bottom Line. It was a club for adults most nights, but once a month, in the summer they threw teen parties I'll never forget. My friends Regina, Stacy, Stephanie, and I would go, and I brought along my younger sister Kim. Since we were the Warren County talent show champions, Stephanie and I loved to challenge other teens with our dance skills. We got a reputation for being the girls that wouldn't back down from a dance battle. Because the club was only open for teens once a month, at other times, all we could do was ride around Henderson and essentially loiter at car washes and gas stations. As I look back on it now, I realize how absolutely ridiculous it was we were riding around town, hanging out in parking lots for fun. My cousins lived in Raleigh, and my parents would let us drive an hour there and hang out. There was plenty to do there, as it was the state capital. We started hanging out at Club Iguana when they initiated a teen night.

I wasn't into getting into trouble. I was the responsible one. I got good grades and was involved in all sorts of extra-curricular activities. I did what I was supposed to do, so my parents let me have free reign. Since Raleigh was one hour away from home, my parents didn't really give me a curfew by the time I was a senior. I'm pretty sure they didn't want me rushing home, which might have caused me to get a speeding ticket or to get into a car accident. As long as we came home before the sun came back up, it was all good in my house.

One particular evening, I took some of my other friends with me to go to Club Iguana. It was my neighbor Chevon, her cousin Casey, my best friend Chandra, as always, my sister Kim, and me. Because I had to take my little sister Kim, I guess my parents figured I couldn't get in too much trouble.

That summer night, the five of us headed to Raleigh. We were meeting my cousin Chante, at Crabtree Valley Mall. We were then going to go to her house and to Club Iguana from there. My cousin was driving in front of us. I was driving my 1995 Nissan 200SX. It was brand new, but a base model. I previously had a dark green 1980 Mercedes 200D. Despite it being unreliable, I didn't care because it was a Mercedes, and I got to ride around playing the song, "Mercedes Boy" by Pebbles. However, because it was unreliable, my mom insisted my dad get me a new car, hence the new Nissan.

I was driving, Casey was my front seat passenger, and Kim was in the back middle in between Chandra and Chevon. We were riding on Interstate 440, which had five lanes on each side, listening to Luke and bouncing to lyrics that even as an adult are still inappropriate. But I'm an honorary south Floridian, so it's in my roots. "Uh uh, get it get it! Uh, uh get it, get it! I wanna rock, I wanna rock, I wanna rock, I wanna rock, I wanna rock!" A car that was getting onto the highway was merging into my lane. I would later learn he didn't see my car, but as he was trying to merge, he almost hit us. I was seventeen years old at this point and only had one year of experience driving. Instead of gracefully turning out of the lane, I pulled on the steering wheel abruptly because otherwise, we were going to get hit. Big mistake! I lost control of the car. My Benz had always required a little more pressure for me to turn the wheel. The new Nissan did not necessitate as much power to steer.

When I tried to regain command of my vehicle, which was swerving to the left, I overcorrected, which caused the car to swerve to the right. I gripped the steering wheel with both hands, while my car drove itself. I held the wheel straight, trying to get it to stop swerving. Bigger mistake! The car turned around 180 degrees to face oncoming traffic. Headlights from other cars beamed into my car, making it difficult for me to see. My heart was running a marathon in my chest, while my mouth stilled, and my eyes widened with panic. We didn't have "The Fast and the Furious" movies at that time, but I'm pretty sure it rivaled a scene from the first movie in the series. Casey was yelling all sorts of expletives next to me. Chandra, the daughter of a preacher, was in the back yelling, "Jesus, Jesus!" Kim said nothing, and Chevon just screamed. No words, just yelling. This all played out in a matter of less than a minute, but in that minute, my brain told me, "We're going to get hit!"

The car rolled to a stop. The radio turned off and everything suddenly got silent. On Interstate 440 on a Saturday night, the highway was packed. To my amazement, no one hit us. All of the cars around us must have slowed down as this was all playing out. I don't think I took a breath that entire minute until I realized we were okay. My hands hurt from gripping the steering wheel so tightly. I gasped, let go of the wheel, and then turned the key in the ignition to see if it would start because when we rolled to a stop, the engine stalled. Surprisingly, it did start. I drove the car off to the side of the road, and we got out. The man that almost brought our lives to an early end had pulled over and gotten out of the car. My cousin, who was watching all of this in her rear-view mirror, had pulled over and gotten out as well.

As the older gentleman approached us, I could see in his eyes the remorse. He was probably the age of my parents, and he ran over yelling, "I'm sorry. I didn't see you." Casey was enraged and looked like he was going to attack the man. "How in the world did you not see us?" He went on to say some other words, but I couldn't hear them. I put my head on the hood of the car and just tried to remember how to breathe normally again. Nickye picked up a crowbar and was ready to swing at any moment.

At some point, all of the yelling stopped, we got back in our respective cars, and we drove to my cousin's house. Once we were sitting in her kitchen, we all replayed our versions of the dramatic scene. Kim still had not said anything. Suddenly, it was as if it had just registered she wasn't dead. She started crying. We coaxed her back into calm, and then for some reason, I couldn't stop laughing.

I looked at Kim and said, "It's an hour later, and now you decide to cry? Where were you this entire time?" We all started cracking up, even Kim. That's how I am about things. We could have been seriously injured, but I found it funny. It was almost as if I was laughing at the Devil because he tried to take us out that night. He was trying to destroy the great purpose God had for me, and God sent His angels to protect us because my car wasn't even scratched. We probably should have gotten in the car and driven to a church, but instead, we drove to Club Iguana and danced off any fears we had. Driving back to Soul City that night, I suddenly felt like I had escaped death. I knew I was destined for amazing things, and the Devil was going to try his best to keep me from being great.

MOMENT OF REFLECTION

Was there ever a time when your life was in danger? What were the circumstances around it? There are various reasons for situations, and sometimes, they are a result of the Devil attempting to hinder your purpose in life. Maybe it could be a result of God wanting to root out certain unGodly characteristics. Consider whether it was God or the Devil that was active in the situation. Reflect on how God's protection kept you safe, regardless of the cause of the scenario. Take time right now to praise God and thank Him for shielding you from harm.

CHAPTER SEVEN

Heal the World

The Lord gave me this answer: "Write down clearly on clay
tablets what I reveal to you, so that it can be read at a glance.
Put it in writing, because it is not yet time for it to come true.
But the time is coming quickly, and what I show you will come
true. It may seem slow in coming, but wait for it; it will
certainly take place, and it will not be delayed."
Habakkuk 2:2-3, GNT

I actually started my career in medicine during high school. In the eleventh grade, I had the opportunity to take a Health Occupations Education class. We learned medical terminology, clinical nursing assistant skills such as how to properly make a bed and how to change the sheets on the bed with a bedridden person lying in the bed, and I learned the circulation of the heart. This was when I became interested in cardiology and thought I wanted to be a cardiovascular surgeon. I changed that thought quickly once I got into medical school.

My instructor, Mrs. George, was a nurse and was also the mother of one of the girls in my clique. Mrs. George was a strict disciplinarian. She did not play when it came to schoolwork, possibly as a result of her African descent. Africans can be known for being stubborn and strict. At the time, we thought she was being hard on us. If I was playing around or talking in class, she wouldn't yell at or embarrass me. She would simply look down her nose at me over her eyeglasses and say in her African accent, "Kellye, are you finished with your work?" I would shake my head "no" and continue on with my studying. Now I know she was only the first of numerous people who would ride me before I got to my end goal, so I appreciate her. Because of her, I was able to accept the various styles of teaching I would later experience and decipher the difference between those who were truly concerned about my education versus those who were strict disciplinarians who couldn't have cared less about whether I passed or failed.

In my senior year, my classmates and I were preparing to be certified as nursing assistants, and we were required to do clinicals in a nursing home. I knew I didn't want to be a nurse, but I also knew I needed to get some experience in the medical field. We worked at Warren Hills, the only nursing home I can recall in our county at the time. The nursing home was no joke. I hated it—the stale smell of urine and elderly people are something you can't forget. As nursing assistants, you get assigned all the menial, nauseating tasks no one wants to do. As a nursing assistant *student*, the nursing assistants get to hand you all the work they typically have to do but don't want to do because they are overworked and underpaid.

I remember having to clean an elderly person's diaper. Up to that point, I hadn't even changed a baby's diaper, so imagine my horror when I saw what was in that diaper. I'm thinking, *I have to clean this person up*? Nickye covered her grossed-out countenance with a mask and donned two pairs of gloves. Being a nursing assistant was kind of horrific to me at that point, but I had a plan, and I was sticking to it.

By the time I graduated from high school, I passed the test to become a Certified Nursing Assistant. The first couple of summers, I worked in the assisted living center in Soul City, which was named after our town's founder. The Floyd B. McKissick Assisted Living Center was pretty nice. It was a newer facility, so it didn't have the typical geriatric resident smell. Because Soul City was so small, it mainly consisted of residents from Warren County. Also, it wasn't filled to the brim with residents like most other assisted living centers or nursing homes.

There were daily planned activities such as Bingo or artwork. My mother did some work with the center, so it was a no-brainer I would get a job there. Besides, nursing assistants are always needed. It wasn't like they were going to turn away people who wanted to work. Sometimes, I had to work night shifts. Most of those nights, I had to work with an obese black nurse that used me to do all the scut work, as she sat at the nurses' station ordering me around.

I don't remember many of the residents there, but one lady, in particular, stands out in my mind. Ms. Parker was suffering from some mild dementia, so I'm not sure if she remembered me from one day to the next, but she loved to talk to me. She was one of a few residents I was assigned to assist first thing in the morning. When I got there, I had to go wake her up and help her get dressed. I wasn't really fond of helping the residents bathe because it could be tedious work, but Ms. Parker always seemed to be able to take care of herself—she didn't have the typical old-person smell either.

I don't know if Ms. Parker had family around because I never saw them, but because she would treat me like I was a grandchild, I felt a connection to her. When I would ask her what she wanted to wear for the day, she would respond, "You pick out something nice for me, will you?" After I decided on her attire, she would go to her jewelry box and pick out a nice bracelet or necklace to wear with it. I thought it was sad she was suffering from dementia. I wanted her to remember our conversations, but day after day, I found myself repeating things I had already told her. One day I told her I was studying to be a doctor. She looked so proud. She got really close to me, and she said barely above a whisper, "You become a doctor, baby. Don't let anything stop you."

She was my first real exposure to someone with dementia. The last summer I worked at the McKissick Center, I saw Ms. Parker's health start to decline. She wasn't able to assist me as well with getting herself dressed for the day, and it disturbed me. Once I got an apartment in college, I didn't go back home for the summers, and I never saw Ms. Parker again, but she left a lasting impression on me. She made me think of my grandfather because he had dementia toward the end of his life. She and my grandfather made me dream that maybe one day I could be the physician to find a way to prevent dementia. As much as I would like to say I'm on the road to making that happen today, the fact of the matter is, I kind of hate research, so I'm not likely to be the one who finds the solution.

My grandfather was always such a reserved man; the strong silent type. However, as he aged, dementia set in. My auntie took care of him, and it had to be an arduous task. When visiting, I could see the toll dementia had taken on him. It was almost as if he reverted to his toddler form. He would need assistance with feeding himself, and he would urinate on the floor. Auntie was livid!

"Daddy, why are you peeing on the floor?"

"I couldn't make it to the bathroom," he'd say.

One time I recall him asking my baby sister to buy him adult diapers. "Kourtnye, go to the store and buy me some Pampers."

Kourtnye was always quite comical, even as a child. "But Grandpa, I can't even drive," was her response.

It was sad to see this child-like version of my grandfather when I could remember him fixing the chain on my bicycle and doing all the other handiwork around the house. His dementia further solidified my wanting to be a doctor so I could change the world. Because I had a vision of being a doctor at such a young age, I did not know anything about writing down my vision. As an adult, I have since learned it is a good idea to have goals readily visible to help me stay on track.

MOMENT OF REFLECTION

Think about visions you've had for your life. Were you able to accomplish them? What helped you or hindered you from achieving these dreams? As I've developed a closer relationship with God, I learned about vision boards. I've created vision boards as a reminder to myself of things I want to accomplish. I encourage you to write down your goals and refer to them regularly as a reminder of what you're working toward, whether it be a vision board or a journal. I have both. My vision board is simply a dry-erase board I have hung in my closet with life goals on it. I use words and pictures of things I am working towards, and I write them or hang them on the board. I use the journal to document where I am in life, so I can read over my entries and see what strides I have made. I urge you to find some way that works for you to stay motivated and pursue your dreams.

CHAPTER EIGHT

Fantasy

We are hard-pressed on every side, yet not crushed; we are perplexed, but not in despair; persecuted, but not forsaken; struck down, but not destroyed---

II Corinthians 4:8-9, NKJV

I grew up watching A&T's band. My dad and Uncle Henry were in A&T's band, and I felt destined to be in the band too. Dr. Johnny B. Hodge was the band director in my day. He was a tall, slender, bald guy with glasses and the bark of a Rottweiler. We called him "Doc." Doc was a no-nonsense kind of guy, who said and did what he wanted. He did not tolerate shenanigans. One time, a member of the percussion section was talking while we were preparing for a football game, and Doc lost it. "Take off my uniform, and get out! Don't come back!" he yelled. That boy had to take his uniform off then and there. I'm glad he had shorts on underneath because I'm pretty sure Doc wouldn't have cared and would have sent the guy out with his underwear on.

Doc liked me though. I knew Doc before I got to A&T because he put on a summer band camp for middle and high school students. I attended for two summers and became close to Doc. He grew up in Vance County, which neighbored my own Warren County. Because of this, we had an instant bond. He would lovingly refer to me as "little girl from Warren County."

Since I was a drum major in high school, there was no way I wasn't going to be leading the band at A&T, or so I thought. I had been molded by probably the best drum major to ever march in Aggie Stadium-Anthony Criss. Anthony, or Ant as everyone called him, was the drum major of all drum majors in A&T history. He had already been chosen to be drum major his freshman year when he first entered the band. Doc saw him in high school at Hillside, in

Durham, North Carolina, and he recruited him to A&T's band specifically to be drum major. He never played his instrument in the marching band; he was drum major the entire time he went to A&T. He was also a solo drum major for some of those years. He even arrived on the field in a helicopter for one half-time performance. He always had the most energy, and one's eyes would easily be drawn to him during the entire field show, despite about 100 other people marching on the same field. He is a legend to this day.

The A&T band camp is where I met Ant. I'll never forget when he saw I could dance. My roommate for band camp was someone I knew from Warren County, Demaura Hawkins. Pretty much everyone in the county knew I could dance, so one day, when we had some downtime, we were walking with our camp counselors, one being Ant. As we were walking and talking, Demaura said to Ant, "Kellye can do some of your moves."

Ant turned around with a questioning glance, "What moves?"

I didn't know she was going to put me on the spot, so I was hesitant, but I never turned down a chance to dance. I broke out one of the steps I had seen him do in the stands at a football game, anxiously seeking his approval. He had the biggest grin on his face, and I instantly knew I had impressed him. He ran over beside me, screaming, "Come on! Do it again!" This time, he did the moves along with me.

From that point on, whenever I went to A&T football games as a high schooler, I would go talk to Ant. He even took me on the track one game so I could dance with him. People in the band were so impressed with me that by the time I actually got to be in A&T's band as a freshman, some of the older band students already knew who I was.

Because Doc was like a surrogate father to me, and since I was unofficially trained by a Blue and Gold Marching Machine legend, I was eagerly awaiting my chance to be drum major. I had the moves. What I didn't know at the time was there are only a select few females who can say they have been HBCU drum majors. The only real reason that holds true is tradition. There are more than enough qualified female leaders, and multiple promising young ladies have tried out for the position, but few have ever crossed the burning sands of the unofficial sorority of female drum majors.

Doc was instrumental in me pledging the band sorority, Tau Beta Sigma National Honorary Band Sorority, otherwise known as TBS. The chapter was preparing to initiate a new line, and Doc wanted me on it. He had one of the members approach me about joining. I hadn't really thought about it at that point, especially since I was a freshman, and I didn't really know what I was getting myself into. But because Doc wanted me to do it, I did it. It was one of the best decisions of my life, and it led to a cascade of events which shaped who I am today. Those ladies taught me how to be a leader. Although I loved a crowd, I still had my shy, reserved side, and they helped me to grow out of it. If I had not pledged TBS, I don't know if I would have had the nerve to even joke about being drum major to Doc.

We were at our last regular game of the season against South Carolina State University, during my sophomore year. I was proud to see they had a female drum major. After the game, we went to a restaurant before taking the journey home from Charlotte to Greensboro. I was sitting with some of my sorority sisters, and we were joking around with Doc. Before pledging TBS, I probably would never have asked Doc this, but I jokingly said, "Hey Doc, when are we going to get a female drum major?" Although I was acting like I was messing around, I really did want to be a drum major. There were no tryouts in my day. Doc chose the drum majors, and that was it. If I wanted to be drum major, the only way it would happen is if he selected me for the position. I didn't know at the time, but there had never been a female drum major there before. Some HBCU bands still haven't had one to this day. Females are still trying to break through that proverbial glass ceiling.

Doc stopped mid-laugh and had the gravest look on his face as he answered, "Never, as long as I'm band director."

I laughed and played it off, but I was instantly crushed. Nickye threw down her mace, which is the metal baton drum majors typically carry, and walked away, dejected. All I ever wanted to be in A&T's band and eventually, to be drum major. Although I figured I would never get the chance to be drum major, I continued to enjoy being in the band. I gave it my all.

The next summer, August 1998, it was time for band camp. Band camp is a grueling week, Sunday to Sunday, of all-day marching and learning music. Camp started the first Sunday afternoon, but Monday morning, it would begin at 5 a.m. and would go until 10:00 p.m., with two-hour breaks for breakfast, lunch, and dinner. Band camp for HBCUs is like a mini-boot camp. We were preparing for band war. We dressed in gold shirts, blue shorts, and combat boots. I was a junior and accustomed to the rigorous routine. That year was going to be different though. The first afternoon, while everyone was piling up in the band room getting instruments, Doc had me step into the chorus room of Frazier Hall. He and the assistant band director Kenny Ruff, were sitting in chairs in the front row. They had me stand in front of them.

I didn't know what was going on. I was instantly nervous, and my legs felt weak. Kenny instructed me to get to attention. I jumped into position. Feet together, arms at my side, chest out.

Kenny yelled, "About Face; About Face!" I started performing the move, but because it was the first day of band camp, and I was beyond terrified at being alone in the room, I messed it up. I had not thought about marching band in months. My brain failed me, and when I tried again, I could not remember the simple movement I had done a million times. I turned to Doc, who was expressionless and said, "I'm sorry. I can't remember how to do the command right now." He looked at me and said matter-of-factly, "Go on back to the band room."

Nickye was jumping up and down, pleading with me to ask for another chance. Meanwhile, I walked slowly back to the band room shaking my head the entire time. I had no idea what that test was about, but I'd failed it. I didn't tell anyone where I had been. I just took my seat and picked up my saxophone. In the back of my mind, I wondered, "What was he testing me for?" Doc entered the band room, and we started rehearsal like the whole debacle never happened.

That afternoon, as we were getting lined up to march to the practice field and work on our field show, the drum majors called the band to attention. "Ten hut; ten hut!"

"A&T!" the band shouted in unison. Everyone was still, waiting for the whistle to start the percussion cadence. But it didn't come. Out of my peripheral vision, I could see Kenny walking to the back of the band. I assumed he was looking to see that everyone was positioned properly at attention. Suddenly, he was right beside me. Without a word, he took my saxophone and grabbed my arm.

My heart started running a marathon in my chest. What did I do? Was I in trouble? Was this because I couldn't remember how to do an About Face? Was he going to embarrass me in front of the band? He placed me in line with the three drum majors, dropped my arm, and with a blank gaze, simply stated, "Give my drum majors some competition." Nickye did a back-handspring ending in a full split, which Kellye can't really do, by the way.

Within seconds, the fear turned into elation. The shock on my face turned into a smile. I looked at the three drum majors, and they were grinning back at me. They had no clue what was going to happen either, but they seemed just as excited as I was for me to be marching with them. I looked over at Doc, who had his poker face on. He simply turned around and started walking down the street. I looked back at the band, and they looked more perplexed than me. This wasn't business as usual. Suddenly a female had a shot. I gazed around at all the women in the band, and the weight of the world hit me like a defensive end sacking a quarterback. I couldn't mess this up, or the crack I had made in the glass ceiling would be sealed up and likely not be cracked for years to come. I had to become a champion for all the women who would come after me.

The head drum major called us to attention again. This time though, I was leading the band and not hanging out in the back. This was really happening. His whistle sounded, and everyone simultaneously started marching, as the percussion section played a cadence. The three official drum majors had a mace, and I didn't. That wasn't going to stop me though. I had been imitating my hero Anthony Criss for years. It was time to stop imitating and become a hero to others. I wasn't used to marching like a drum major. I was used to marching like a saxophone player. That wasn't a problem for me though. As a freshman, I learned you have to catch on to some of the techniques without formal instruction. As we marched, the section leader yelled, "Catch it!" You had to replicate the moves they were doing. This was survival of the fittest. Figure it out, or look ridiculous while everyone else marched as one.

As the three drum majors were moving in sync, I began to move like them. When they did something unfamiliar to me, I didn't let it get me down. Eventually, I would "catch it." By the time we got down to the practice field, I was beginning to look like one of the guys. The drum majors put their maces up to signal to the percussion to kick down or to stop the cadence, and I put my arms up as if I had a mace. The whistle blew. *Tweeeeeeeeeeet, tweet, tweet, tweet, tweet!* The band answered, "Long halt, long halt, one, two, three, kick down!"

We all stopped. We waited for the moment when Kenny gave us permission to get at ease. When that time came, the biggest smile appeared on my face. The three drum majors came over to congratulate me. Then other band members came over to do the same. I looked to Doc, and once again, there was no expression to let me know if I was failing horribly or if there was hope for me, but if this was going to be the only time I got to march as drum major, I made the most of it. Doc didn't tell me to get back to my section, so I stayed with the drum majors for the rest of practice.

The next day, I arrived at practice almost expecting to be demoted back to my section, but I wasn't. I had a new position as drum major. The first day and a half of band camp, the drum majors were our own trainers. Since we initially did not have any of the former band members in our positions, "old heads" came to help us. It wasn't unusual for former band members to help out during band camp. Old heads from the percussion section and auxiliary were frequently in attendance, despite no longer being in the band. I thought things would get easy, but along came Jimmie Wright. He had been a drum major back in the 80s and was very dedicated to tradition. I hadn't seen him at band camp the previous two years, but suddenly, he was there. I didn't know why, but it didn't take long for me to figure it out. He was trying to break me, or so I thought. Doc gladly let Jimmie take over the reins, training the drum majors, while he tended to the rest of the band.

At the time, I wasn't sure if he'd decided to come because he heard Doc was letting a female be drum major or if it had always been his plan, but I got the distinct feeling he wasn't happy with me being given this opportunity. Later in life, I would find out that Jimmie tried to break anyone that was a drum major and not just me because I was a female. He was an equal opportunity drill sergeant when it came to training drum majors throughout the years. He later commented on a Facebook post, when other former drum majors were giving him a hard time about his vigorous coaching, "I thought y'all wanted to be good."

Jimmie gave us pure hell. He made us march for hours. When we messed up, we had to run laps. When we marched down to the practice field, we made the band run laps if we heard them talking while we were in formation. Jimmie said to all of us drum majors, "Y'all were messing around too. So that's eight laps for y'all." Our mouths all dropped. Nickye passed out.

We had only given the band two laps. He gave us eight laps around the practice field, which is basically the same size as the football field. That meant almost two miles. I quickly figured out I wasn't as in shape as I thought I was. At lap four, my lungs felt like they were on fire. I started breathing rapidly, my legs felt like Jell-O, and I was sure I was going to pass out at any minute. I was trying so hard, but I felt like the other guys were being punished for my being female. They wouldn't have been treated this way if I was a dude, I thought. I was slowing the guys down because I felt like I'd suddenly developed asthma.

They reduced speed for me, and one of them, Mitch, even offered to run with me on his back so I could rest. I contemplated allowing him to carry me the rest of the way. That's when I made a conscious decision: I wasn't going to let my body shut down on me. Nor would I let Jimmie have the satisfaction of proving I didn't have what it took to honor the position I was blessed to hold. With the last bit of wind I had in me, I told him, "I......can...do...this." I kept going, and we eventually finished our laps. I collapsed onto the ground. Jimmie had a smirk on his face.

I only had a few minutes before our break was over, and we had to continue learning our first field show of the season. As I got up off the ground, I suddenly felt like I'd gained an extra fifty pounds. I made it through practice and was so thankful when we were done for the night. My roommate and college best friend, Shoba, drove us home in my car after rehearsal because she sensed the agony in me. As I sat in the car for the twelve-minute drive to our residence, all my muscles tensed up so badly I became immobile. When Shoba parked the car at our apartment, I couldn't move. She looked at me as if to say, "We're home." Out of my peripheral vision, because I felt my head would fall off if I turned my neck, I could feel her looking at me, and then I told her, "I don't think I can make it up the steps."

I knew she wouldn't be able to carry me, so it was either, I tell my body to get over itself or I was going to sleep in the car. Sleeping in the car was not even an option, so I picked one leg up using my arms and hands to physically lift it and pushed it out of the car, then followed it with the other, and before long, I'd made it out of the vehicle. My greatest challenge was up ahead though—the steps. I stood looking at the ten steps, and at that moment, I felt like I had ten flights to climb. I was exhausted. My muscle's muscles ached. Parts of me I didn't know existed made an appearance just to bring suffering to my body. I could barely keep my thin frame upright. I made an alarmingly unbearable first step, and my back responded by spasming. I bent over and got on my hands and knees, and painfully, slowly, I climbed up the concrete steps. One by one, I ascended each stair, my knees scraping over the concrete edges, leaving behind tiny particles of skin.

Now I had abrasions, which added a new source of discomfort. I had to pray my way up those steps. Once inside, I took a hot bath and stayed in there until the water had soothed my aching limbs and back. I had blisters on the back of my ankles from rubbing against my combat boots. I had never experienced that kind of total body torture before. Because it took so long for me to get in my apartment and out of the bathtub, I didn't get to bed until midnight.

The next morning, the pain was worse. As I tried to get out of bed, I cried out and crashed to the floor, which only amplified the suffering. We had to be at band camp at 5:00 a.m. I had slept a total of four hours, but my body was so weary, it felt like I'd slept four minutes. The stairs of my apartment were again troublesome, but I sat down and slid down the ten steps. When I got to practice, we stretched to warm up. Every movement felt like I was tearing muscle fibers. I was not going to show anyone how much pain I was in, so I gritted my teeth and endured in silence. When we were done stretching, the band would run two laps around the parking lot. I wasn't sure I was going to be able to make it, but as I powered forward, begging my body to yield, my muscles started to loosen up, and I no longer felt like I was being ripped apart.

Jimmie wasn't there for the morning portion of practice, but he was there in the afternoon, ready to inflict more misery on us, but mainly on me. As we were taking a break, Jimmie started yelling at us about how we weren't together, and we needed more work. One of the drum majors, Chris, was yelling back at him. I attempted to give my opinion, and Jimmie snapped, "I don't even know why you're talking; you're not even drum major yet."

I halted mid-sentence. Nickye was so stunned she didn't even have a retort. I felt like crying. No one in my life up to that point had been so cruel to me, so the harsh reality that someone didn't care about my feelings was almost too much to withstand in my physically and emotionally weakened state. I couldn't get this close to being drum major to have it all taken away from me. I didn't know if what he'd said was true. He had been talking to Doc. Maybe Doc hadn't made his final decision about me being drum major. Perhaps I was still in trial mode, and if I made one wrong step, all my hopes and dreams would be crushed into little tiny figments of my imagination. I didn't finish my sentence, but Chris spoke up for me.

"We *do* know she's drum major, and you don't have any say-so in that."

I relaxed a little, but the guys kept arguing until Jimmie realized the three drum majors were on my side. I don't know if that's what stopped the argument or if he just began to understand how we were losing precious practice time, but we got back to working on our marching style. The rest of band camp was uneventful, as I caught on to all the moves and began to blend in with the fellas. Jimmie was no longer pestering us, and I began to feel at ease as the full realization of earning the title of first female drum major dawned on me. The revelation I was the first came from one of the percussionists, Terrell. He mentioned it on the practice field one day.

"You know you're the first female in our band's history, right?"

I was dumbfounded. "Are you serious?"

Another band member interjected, "I think we had one before."

Terrell was adamant though, and eventually, someone confirmed that although a few females tried out, one was never chosen. Suddenly, I understood the gravity of the whole situation. I made history, or like some people like to call it, her-story. It was awesome to know, but I didn't really appreciate that declaration until later in life.

During practice, the drum majors wore the band's typical blue and gold apparel with combat boots, but we also had blue and gold striped socks that came up to just below our knees, mesh see-through football jerseys over our gold shirts, and blue visors. One day, Ant came to practice and saw I had on the unofficial drum major practice uniform. He abruptly halted and smiled so hard; I could have counted all his teeth. He said, "No?!"

I matched his smile with all my teeth and answered, "Yes!"

He came running toward me and hugged me so tightly I thought I would suffocate. That was the second greatest moment of becoming a drum major that year. The greatest moment came the first time I got to perform. It was the Aggie-Eagle Classic, a rivalry game between us and North Carolina Central University, another HBCU. This rivalry went back years, as the two schools are fifty-five miles apart. It was Labor Day weekend, 1998. So many people would come to this game that we held it at Carter-Finley Stadium, a bigger stadium in Raleigh, owned by North Carolina State University. Between the two schools, the game was always sold out, and the seating capacity was a little over 50,000 people. It's unfortunate neither of our stadiums could hold that many people because NC State got to profit off the smaller HBCUs, but we had to do what we had to do.

The temperature was somewhere in the upper 90s. I had on my drum major uniform for the first time that season. Although the uniform weighed five pounds itself and was trapping every degree of heat in the atmosphere, I didn't care. This would be the first time I was revealed to the HBCU marching band world as a drum major. Whatever I did that day would go down in her-story. I was ready though. I craved the crowd like a baby needs milk. Marching into the stadium, all the drum majors had on the humongous tall hats, which added another pound, so no one could tell I was a female. I had a short Halle Berry-like haircut, and I've always been skinny, so it wasn't like I had much of a figure underneath the uniform, hence the reason one couldn't tell I was female when I had the hat on. Once it was off, my face and hair were visible, and then it was apparent. The guys always shaved their heads for the first games. When we were seated in the stands, we took our hats off, but the focus was on the bands playing back and forth and not on me...yet.

When halftime came, it was on! We typically lined up on the sideline about four minutes before the end of the quarter. While standing there, waiting for the clock to tick down to 0:00, signaling the end of the first half, my mouth was dry, and my heart was beating twice its normal rate. I was anxious but not in a bad kind of way. I was ready to prove to the marching band world I was better than many male drum majors out there. When we stepped onto the field, the announcer did his typical speech, "Introducing the 1998 edition of the Blue and Gold Marching Machine, under the direction of Dr. Johnny B. Hodge." He went on to give more pleasantries and then the moment came, "Introducing the first female drum major in A&T history!" Nickye had her popcorn in hand, ready to watch the performance. That was my cue. Before the game, I spoke with the percussion section and told them to give me a drum roll while I saluted the crowd. The rest of the band had no clue what I was about to do, with the exception of my fellow drum majors.

I planted the pointy end of my mace in the ground so it would stand alone without me, I turned around, took a deep breath, then as fast as I could, I relived my track days by sprinting to the middle of the field, jumped up in the air, came down in a split, and popped back up with a celebratory fist pump in the air, then ran back to retrieve my mace and get the Marching Machine cranked up. As I ran back, I looked around at the crowd, and from what I could see, I had probably 90% of the audience on their feet. People from the rival school even stood up and applauded. Nickye jumped out of her seat so abruptly to clap, she dropped her popcorn. It's generally understood that female drum majors are unicorns in the HBCU world, and the fact that we were rivals didn't mean people didn't appreciate the importance of the situation. The joy I felt in that moment was like none before. My name would forever be in the history books. I opened the doors for others. People might not remember my name, but they would remember that moment.

Before we blew the whistle to signal the start of the show, I looked at the band members and they looked ready for war like they couldn't wait to perform. That's what we did. That's what we always did. We gave the people what they wanted. When we got off the field, many of the band members (especially the females) told me how my introduction got them hyped. After we marched back into the stands and kicked down so we could drink our Gatorades and take a break, people were giving me high-fives and saying how well I did.

Unfortunately, in the twenty years since I graduated, there has only been one other female drum major. To this day, I march with the alumni band and people say, "You still got it, girl!" The feeling of empowerment I obtained in that position was like no other. Years later, after Dr. Hodge retired and we were speaking candidly, he told me that when people found out he chose a female to be drum major, people would call his house and hang up. It wasn't like he received death threats, but his peace was disrupted.

It all stopped after people saw me perform. I silenced the naysayers and the haters and made it okay for young ladies to follow me. I proved everyone wrong who felt like there was no way a woman could perform like a man. I'm glad I represented Doc well, and I'm forever grateful for the guidance he gave me. Years later, after I had graduated, I asked Doc what made him change his mind about a female drum major. He said in his loud and boisterous way, "I knew you could be the baddest b**** out there!" It sounds harsh, but he meant it as a compliment. Somewhere in the time from me joking around with Doc about picking a female drum major and band camp the following year, I made him look at me differently. When mentoring young ladies presently, that's what I tell them. We can do more than we can even imagine. We can't fall into the trap set by the less progressive males in our society telling us to stay in our lane. We have to speak up and speak out and make them listen and acknowledge us. Even if no other woman has done what you want to do, believe that you could be the first, and *prove it*!

The funny thing is, one of my Biology professors could have halted my band career even before it began. That story goes something like this. It was orientation day at A&T. All of the Biology freshman students had to come to the department to meet their advisors. I was super excited because, after multiple years of being on campus as an Aggie legacy, I was finally a student. I stood with other new students in the lobby of the Biology building, Barnes Hall, while the professors and department chair were there to greet and guide us. I met one of the Zoology professors, Mr. Williams. He took a look at my schedule and frowned. I was instantly concerned, as I didn't know what he'd found wrong with my course load.

"You're going to have to quit the band," he told me.

Nickye was already trying on band uniforms, so she stopped immediately to gaze back at him and return his frown with hands on her hips in a defiant stance.

I wanted to be sure I heard him correctly. "Excuse me?"

"You want to be a doctor, correct?"

"Yes," I proudly declared.

"The band practices too many hours. You won't have time to study."

Despite being a freshman walking into the building for the first time, I was confident enough in myself that his doubt fueled me, so I responded, "If I see my grades are slipping because of the band, I'll make the decision to quit. Until then, I'll be marching in the band."

Nickye resumed putting on the band uniform and started marching toward Mr. Williams, playing her saxophone loudly. Sometimes bold statements like that would just roll right off my tongue without a thought. I would later understand that when I made such striking statements, it was a message from God that I was on the right path.

He looked back at me with a smirk and said, "Okay. You'll see."

Well, he saw. Not only did I stay in the band all four years, but I became a history-maker in the process, and I also got into medical school, likely with the assistance of my title of "First Female Drum Major."

A&T's first female Drum Major

MOMENT OF REFLECTION

In life, people may not always be rooting for you to succeed. Sometimes, they will actually try to hinder you or convince you that you can't do something. It's up to you to assess whether your goal is achievable. However, it's my firm conviction, if it's in God's will, you can achieve whatever you believe. What are some ways you can continue to fight even when all the odds seem to be against you? Find your own scriptures to motivate you in times of trials, and place them somewhere visible.

CHAPTER NINE

Survivor

When pride comes, then comes shame;
But with the humble is wisdom.
Proverbs 11:2, NKJV

Even though I got into medical school the first time I applied, I know it was by the grace of God. I tell my mentees to this day not to get into medical school the way I did. For instance, I didn't prepare long or hard for the MCAT. Between my junior and senior years at A&T, I went to the Medical Education Development (MED) program at the University of North Carolina at Chapel Hill. See. I eventually went to UNC-CH as Ms. Baker wanted me to, but only for a brief period, and on my own terms. HA! The program was for six weeks during the summer, and it was designed for minority and underrepresented students to get a taste of medical school. They crammed the first year of medical school into that summer, and they also provided MCAT preparation. Because of this, I figured I would just use the program to help me study for the MCAT. The problem was, I was focusing so intently on passing the core curriculum classes of the MED program, there wasn't much time left to study for anything else.

The MCAT prep was done on Saturdays during the program, so I used the week to study for my summer courses and used the weekend to study for the MCAT. Once the program was over, I had two weeks of free time before band camp started and then one week before school started. I would say I probably studied a good three weeks for the MCAT. I scored the absolute minimum I needed to get into medical school, which is why I don't recommend doing what I did. But God had a plan for me.

I graduated from A&T with a 3.4 GPA, and I believe the reason I got into medical school had to do in part with me being the first female drum major. When applying for medical school, I wrote about this in my personal statement, and it was the focus of two out of three of my interviews at the Brody School of Medicine at East Carolina University (ECU), where I would eventually attend. It showed them I could overcome adversity, which is what I believe helps minorities get into medical school. In college, I was involved in numerous activities that helped to counteract the fact I wasn't a 4.0 student like many of my medical school classmates. I studied in college, but I was able to rely on my natural intellect and my ability to cram vital information at the last minute. Don't get me wrong, I was studious, and my sorority sisters will be the first to tell you, that at step practice, I had a book in my hand while waiting for everyone to show up. On band trips, while most people were sleeping, I was reviewing class lecture notes. It wasn't like I didn't study, but I could have studied harder and more efficiently.

That's why medical school was an eye-opener. First of all, being at a predominantly white institution was a different world. I had gone to predominantly black schools my entire life. I don't see this as a negative, but it was a culture shock for me. To be honest, I hated being at ECU. I didn't hate the school itself, but I often felt like I didn't fit in. I had never had that feeling before. As I stated in earlier chapters, I was involved in everything early in life. I was a "Jill of all trades": student, athlete, musician, dancer, singer. In medical school, nobody cared about any of that. Many people see doctors as just highly educated people with the kind of focus that prevents them from achieving anything other than scholastics. For many of my classmates, that was their truth, and they had little interest in other things. Most of my classmates didn't care that I was in the history books at A&T because most of them couldn't relate to the HBCU experience. If it wasn't for the Student National Medical Association, I would have been lost. This student group was fashioned after the National Medical Association, which is a medical professional organization designed specifically for minority providers. In this group, many of us had gone to HBCUs, and many of us were in fraternities or sororities. They helped me find my place at ECU.

I did become close with some non-black classmates. For instance, my study buddy Jocelyn Wittstein was my med school angel. Jocelyn was about my height and nearly my same build. She was a lighthearted spirit, and she stood out from our peers in that she didn't automatically see race. In her world, we all were equal.

In Gross Anatomy, our class was divided up by last name, and there were four students to a cadaver. Most class sizes were seventy-two, but we had two students who were held over from the previous class for various reasons. Therefore, we had seventy-four, which meant the last cadaver only had two students. I felt like I was set up for failure from the beginning because instead of making it a little more even by having the last two cadavers with three students each, Jocelyn and I were left as a pair to do all the dissecting on one cadaver.

This actually worked in my favor though. I am a hands-on learner, and I needed to do the work to be able to retain the information. Luckily, Jocelyn was a great partner. Not only that, she became a lifelong friend. Because we were forced to work together so closely in Gross Anatomy, we started studying most subjects together. I'm glad the Lord put her in my path. I could have been partnered with a privileged person who blamed affirmative action as their reason for not achieving certain things, like some of my other classmates. She was so easy-going and genuinely into knowing people regardless of their race.

I overheard some of my white classmates having a conversation one day. I don't know if they didn't realize I could hear them or if they just didn't care, but one of the girls said, "I didn't get into medical school my first time because ECU wants the classes to be more diverse." When I heard this, Nickye proceeded to get dressed in a "Young, Black, and Educated" t-shirt and put on an afro wig in protest. Nickye wanted to barge into their conversation and say, "Do you blame the 75% of non-minority students for keeping you out of med school on your first try? The numbers are still in your favor even if affirmative action is the reason some minorities got in." Honestly, Kellye wanted to say that too.

While I could feel the anger creeping from my toenails to my mouth, and my neck was starting to tense up, preparing to do the "oh-no-you-didn't" black girl head roll, I walked away. Nickye didn't walk away; she was in the girl's face pointing and insulting. I was instantly on edge. I suddenly realized my talent and charm were no longer going to be admired. That girl's ignorant comment made me doubt myself, and it didn't help I was no longer looked at as one of the smarter people in my classes.

At A&T, I was typically leading the curve or right there with the leader, so to suddenly be at the bottom was unsettling for me. I struggled through medical school. I learned I hadn't perfected the art of studying in college. I had to revamp the way I approached studying, and it took some time. It took some humility too. I did okay my first year of medical school because I had been taught a lot of the information in the MED program. My second year, however, I began to struggle. In my third year, I began to doubt whether I was good enough to survive. I tried studying longer hours, but I found the longer I tried reading over the syllabi, the less I retained. I tried writing notes out on index cards, thinking drawing diagrams and pictures would help me remember more, but when I didn't understand some of the concepts, all I was doing was creating pretty artwork I would stare at unproductively.

We started doing our clinical rotations during the third year, and I had surgery as my first rotation, which was the most difficult of all. It was the first time I had ever been in a hospital setting, and it was when my failure started. Mind you, I had failed a couple of tests before. Who hadn't? We all have to mess up here and there for one reason or another, but I had failed a major test this time. In order to pass the rotation, I had to pass a standardized exam, and initially, I didn't. I was flagged as needing "extra assistance." Insert Virginia Hardy.

Virginia was the person people went to for what I perceived as remedial assistance. She was the student services advisor. She was not someone I wanted to visit. Don't get me wrong. She's a great person and a fellow Delta Sigma Theta Sorority sister, but I was going to see her because I was at risk of failure. It was a new position for me. Frankly, I felt dumb. There was no other way to describe it.

Though my instructional time with her would initially be difficult, I instantly liked her when I met her. The first time I walked into the Student Affairs Office, during orientation, she seemed so friendly. Walking into her office, I remember seeing an elephant on her bookshelf, the symbol we use as our unofficial mascot in Delta Sigma Theta.

"Does that elephant mean anything to you?" I asked with the suspicion that she might be my sorority sister.

She smiled knowingly, "Why, yes. It does."

"Soror?" I questioned.

"Yes ma'am!" We quickly embraced.

The student assistance encounter proved to be nothing like our first introduction. Because I was forced to go see Virginia due to academic issues, I was resistant to opening up. My initial consultation with her was icy, to say the least. I was very standoffish. Virginia presented a plan of action to help me become better at test-taking. She wasn't one of the professors, and she wasn't a tutor. She didn't have a medical background, but her job was to find the root cause of my inability to perform at the level of my peers.

We started off doing test questions which had nothing to do with medicine. The questions were basic knowledge questions, almost like SAT prep questions. That in itself was insulting to me because I looked at her as if she was questioning my basic intellect. I remember her presenting me with a question to which I believed I should have known the answer. It was a multiple-choice question where one of the answers was incorrect. The question was:

Which of these words does not mean ebullient?

    a. Buoyant

    b. Jaunty

    c. Depressed

    d. Irrepressible

I got the answer wrong.

In her soothing voice, Virginia asked me, "So what is the question asking you?"

With an angry black woman attitude, I responded, "It's asking me which of these words is wrong."

Without appearing aggravated, she asked, "So what does ebullient mean?"

I hesitated because I didn't know what the word meant. Nickye looked the other way as if to say, "Don't ask me!" Not only did I not know what the word meant, but Virginia had suddenly succeeded at making me feel inferior. She didn't mean to do it, and she didn't know she did it, but she had. Up to this point, when people would try to break me, they couldn't because I felt like I was smarter or better than them in some fashion. But Virginia made me realize I wasn't as book smart as many of my classmates. That's why I had an attitude. A medical school student is supposed to know what a word like ebullient means. All in a heartbeat, I was broken down to a scared little girl. I no longer felt confident, and I started questioning whether I wanted to continue on. I looked down at the paper with the question on it, the one question that almost changed the complete trajectory of my life, and then I looked back up at Virginia and spoke just a decibel above a whisper, "I don't know what it means."

My eyes began to water, and I felt my nose burning with mucus, ready to run. I did not want to show any emotion. Nickye was pleading with me to woman-up. The ability to conceal my true feelings is what kept me strong all those years. Whatever fears I'd had in the past, I was always able to disguise them and fight through them. I couldn't wrangle the fear this time. Fear was like an undefeated heavyweight fighter, and it had me against the ropes, ready to deliver the final blow, which would knock me to the ring floor.

Virginia halted, abruptly, and I felt her sympathy, but it felt like pity. Pity was worse than an insult to me. She didn't answer immediately, and I figured it was because she didn't know how to proceed. Saying the wrong thing might have made me quit medical school, and I'm sure she sensed it. We had more time left in our session that day, but she closed my test booklet and reached for my hand. "It's okay that you don't know the answer. My job is to give you the support you need, however you need it."

We stopped there. When I went home, I cried so hard, my eyes almost swelled shut, my nose resembled Rudolph the Red-Nosed Reindeer, and my body shook violently as I gasped and sniffled. It was ugly crying, like the scenes in the movies where you are in the shower, on the floor, letting the water beat down on you, as you contemplate the meaning of life. For the first time in my life, I questioned my intelligence. That night, I pondered what would happen if I quit medical school, and it occurred to me I didn't have another plan. If I failed at this, all of the time I'd spent was a waste. I prayed and found resilience unlike I had experienced before. Mark 11:23, KJV, became my scripture to live by: "For verily I say unto you, That whosoever shall say unto this mountain, Be thou removed, and be thou cast into the sea; and shall not doubt in his heart, but shall believe that those things which he saith shall come to pass; he shall have whatsoever he saith." Destiny's Child's song "Survivor" became my medical school anthem. If I started to feel I couldn't handle the pressure, I would turn it on and dance like I was one of their background dancers.

Whenever I feel like I'm failing at something, I give myself one good day of throwing myself a pity party. Nickye doesn't like sadness, so she refuses to attend. I just allow myself to feel all the emotions I want to suppress in front of everyone else. Twenty-four hours is all I allow. Then I suck it up and decide whether I am ready to give up and move on or if I'm going to resume fighting. The answer is always, keep battling. I hate losing, and I absolutely loathe giving up. So once the twenty-four hours is done, I let Nickye back in, and we double down on the mission.

The next time I met with Virginia, I had a new sense of determination. Because I previously left her office feeling vulnerable and exposed, I was even frostier than our first visit. That is how I handled people who doubt me. I put up a steel wall so my fragile core would not be revealed. But instead of doubt, Virginia appeared as determined as I was. Somehow, she was able to make me smile when everything inside me was resistant to presenting anything other than strength. We had a limited number of sessions, so she basically counseled me on the tools of effective test-taking. The information wasn't necessarily what confused me a lot of times but the way the test questions were worded. I discovered even the answers I knew, I got wrong because I wasn't taking the time to actually understand what the question was asking. I was also taught how to work my way through a question, even if I didn't know the answer. For example, typically there is a standard format to multiple-choice questions. There's the right answer, a completely wrong answer, two similar answers, and a distractor, which is an almost right answer. Virginia helped me realize I picked the distractor many of the times I got a question wrong.

Virginia changed me. To go from instant affection to almost disdain when I had to meet with her for study skills and test-taking strategies, back to love and affection, was quite a journey. It was all worth it though. She helped me to figure out where my weaknesses were. She helped me develop into a more effective studier. She also became someone I could confide in when I started to waver in confidence.

Virginia was another of the many people who made me who I am today. I only had to do about four or five sessions with her before I was on my own again. However, Virginia was always around if I needed her. She was not only a resource for all medical students, but she was also the advisor for the Student National Medical Association. Being minorities attempting to diversify medicine, she helped us all feel like we belonged in the field, despite the limited number of African American physicians. I believe God brought her into my life because I needed someone I could relate to and receive instruction from. If it had been someone else who made me realize I needed help learning how to prepare for tests, I may have taken offense and blamed race or gender for feeling like I was being singled out. Thank God for Virginia.

MOMENT OF REFLECTION

When a person is prideful, they often cannot receive things such as advice, critiques, or even gifts from other people. Pride causes people to turn away from others, thinking they can handle things on their own. How does pride affect your thoughts and actions? Are you letting *you* get in your way? Ask God to help you receive humility, so you can in return receive all the grace, mercy, and favor He has for you.

CHAPTER TEN

The Proud

God is our refuge and strength [mighty and impenetrable],
A very present and well-proved help in trouble. Therefore we will
not fear, though the earth should change And though the mountains
be shaken and slip into the heart of the seas, Though its waters roar
and foam, Though the mountains tremble at its roaring. Selah.

Psalm 46:1-3, AMP

There is a day in the history of the United States that has specific meanings and memories for everyone. For me, this day happened during my second year of medical school. I was still far from being a doctor but one step closer. We were in our lecture room, and normally, my self-diagnosed ADD would make it so I could hardly focus, but the Psychiatry class that morning was not a lecture as it typically would be. There was a schizophrenic patient who agreed to talk to our class. Sitting there watching her, I admired her bravery. Psychiatric illnesses are often not looked at like other medical illnesses. People frequently view these illnesses as people being "crazy" or "unable to cope with life." That schizophrenic patient, Debra, gave us a glimpse into her world, and it made me hope I would never have to be responsible for anyone like her on a personal level, simply because the disease is not only devastating to the patient, but it can hinder the life of the caretaker as well.

Dr. Michaels was the psychiatrist who taught the lectures. He sat in a chair at the front of the room while Debra was seated across from him. He gave us a brief introduction to her, "This is one of my patients, and she has agreed to tell a little about her story and her illness. She has worked hard to overcome the obstacles that come with her illness, and I think she will make you see schizophrenia in a different way. Debra, if you would just tell us a little about your background."

Debra looked surprisingly calm. I had always imagined psychiatric patients being out of control and disheveled. While there was nothing memorable about what she was wearing or her appearance overall, her words were striking to me. As she discussed her background, I became immersed in her story. "Things got so bad, and nobody knew until I would go missing for days at a time. I started to change in my twenties, and my friends didn't understand what was happening. My apartment was a mess, so I never invited anyone over. I started hearing voices, and I thought they were being transmitted through the airwaves. I put aluminum foil up because I thought, by doing that, I was blocking the radio transmissions that allowed the voices in."

I was literally sitting on the edge of my seat because I was so interested in what she had to say. But then, I became distracted because as she was talking, one of my classmates got up and quickly walked out of the room. I didn't initially think anything of it, but then two more of my classmates walked out. Then another. By that point, I was appalled. Debra could have been anywhere, but she came to give us insight into her disorder, and my rude classmates were walking out of class! I was secretly afraid all the commotion in the classroom was going to set her off and send her into a mental breakdown. Why wouldn't they just sit still and be respectful of Debra? It couldn't have been easy for her to discuss her life in front of a lecture room of strangers.

Once class was over, I walked out of the lecture room shaking my head at the audacity of some of my classmates. I was heated. I walked by the Media Room and saw the television screen showing the World Trade Center's two towers on fire. The two people stationed in the room didn't even notice me staring over their shoulders. "What happened?" I asked.

Without looking my way, one of them answered, "New York has been attacked!"

He kept watching the television, and it was clear I wasn't going to get answers from either of them. I watched a little longer, then looked at my watch, realizing we only had a ten-minute break before our next lecture.

As I took my seat, I could see my classmate, Sean, visibly disturbed. Then it dawned on me...he was from New York. He was one of the people who stepped out of the room while Debra was talking. He kept trying to call someone, and apparently, they weren't answering. When he put the phone down and started collecting his things, I asked, "Is your family okay?" He shook his head. "My sister works in Manhattan, and I can't reach her."

As I was trying to figure out what would be the right thing to say at that moment, Dr. Michaels interjected, "Can I have everyone's attention?"

All eyes turned toward Dr. Michaels. "It has been brought to my attention there has been a tragedy in New York, and I know some of you may be trying to reach your loved ones. We're going to cancel classes for the rest of the day. I'll stay around here if any of you need to talk. You're excused."

Sean had already packed his bag and ran out of the room. I then understood why people had walked out of class earlier. I felt remorse for calling them inconsiderate and all sorts of not-so-nice adjectives before. At the same time, relief flooded over because I didn't have any close family or friends that I knew of in New York.

When I arrived back at my apartment, I should have used the time off to study, since we had exams the next week, but I wanted to see what was happening in New York. I didn't typically watch the news back then, but I flipped back and forth from CNN, MSNBC, and Fox News that day. I couldn't get enough of the coverage. It was like an addiction. The news channels kept replaying the airplanes crashing into the Twin Towers. Although my family wasn't closely affected, sorrow crept over me as more and more information came in. One person reported, "People are jumping from the windows of the building!" To think of having to make a decision between burning in a fire and leaping to sudden death was unreal to me.

I gave myself permission to keep watching all day. I told myself, "Forget about exams," I was dealing with a real tragedy. I stayed up half the night watching the news coverage. I felt I was going to miss something if I went to sleep. When I finally did go to sleep, it was practically time to wake up and go to class again.

For the first few days after the attack, I couldn't wait to go back to my apartment so I could see what the latest news was; hoping for miracles like someone being trapped for hours and days being found alive with only minor injuries. I remember seeing paramedics and doctors working their shifts, then going to Ground Zero after their shifts were over to volunteer. That's when the idea of being an emergency physician became my top priority. I wanted to be a cardiothoracic surgeon at one point and even shadowed one when I was in college, but 9/11 solidified a new path for me. I saw doctors being interviewed. Some were surgeons, but many were emergency physicians. I kept thinking, if anything like this happened again, I wanted to be a part of it. I wanted to be one of those physicians being interviewed by the news crews. I wanted to be able to say I saved someone's life. From that point on, I was certain that emergency medicine was the specialty I would pursue.

MOMENT OF REFLECTION

Tragedies in life are bound to happen. There is nothing we can do to prevent them. The question is, are you going to allow calamity to hinder you or help you? How can you turn your negative thoughts into thoughts of positivity and hope? It's hard to look at the good when there is so much bad, but I encourage you to find your silver lining. Out of the destruction of 9/11, I made a decision to be an emergency physician. What decisions have you made as a result of a negative or dramatic situation in your life? The next time chaos is wreaking havoc on your life, dig deep to turn the negative into a positive. Realize you still have life and God has much greater in store for you.

CHAPTER ELEVEN

Fighter

*Be sober, be vigilant; because your adversary the devil walks
about like a roaring lion, seeking whom he may devour. Resist
him, steadfast in the faith, knowing that the same sufferings
are experienced by your brotherhood in the world.*

1 Peter 5:8-9, NKJV

As I stated earlier, my first clinical rotation ever was surgery. I started off with two weeks of Trauma; this was my first exposure to playing the role of doctor. Medical students weren't expected to make any life-altering choices, but we still had to work like we had significant responsibilities. I had never worked in a hospital setting before. I was in the first two weeks of my eight weeks of surgery, and I'll never forget the first morning of my rotation. It was the summer of 2002, and I was expected to be there at six in the morning. I was rounding in the trauma ICU. The previous day, I had been assigned a patient, and when I walked into the room, I was shocked because he was a twenty-five-year-old who had been involved in a serious motor vehicle accident and had been put on a ventilator. He had malignant hyperthermia, so his vital signs were all over the place. He couldn't talk because he wasn't responsive and had been sedated so he wouldn't breathe over the ventilator.

The room was silent, except for the beeping of the monitors and ventilator. I wasn't prepared for this. I had never worked with a real patient before, and the simulated patients always talked back to me, so I was clueless as to how to perform a history and physical exam on someone who was unresponsive. I walked back out of the room and looked around for anyone who could help me. I met Brian, a surgery intern. As I reflect back on him now, he reminds me of McDreamy on *Grey's Anatomy*, although that time frame pre-dates *Grey's*. He was a handsome guy with dark hair and a calm demeanor; he was new to surgery as well, but he was the only person I saw at that moment who looked like he knew what he was doing. I introduced myself and told him it was my first day of rotations and I didn't know what I was supposed to do. He gave me a brief tour of the ICU, and then I asked him how I was supposed to examine an uncommunicative person. He had his own patients to take care of, but he graciously assisted me.

I would later understand being nice was considered a weakness when it came to being a surgeon. The trauma attendings did everything they could to break Brian. When we had our morning rounds, the attendings would ask the residents questions, and they seemed to grill Brian extra hard. They were relentless, like sharks searching for blood. When they asked him a question he couldn't answer, that was the first drop of blood in the ocean, and the sharks set in motion his slow death as they devoured every piece of him. Little did I know, I would have the same experience myself, as a resident. Brian was my first exposure to the cruelty I would be subjected to as my learning continued. Every resident got their share of unwanted attention from the attendings, but those that seemed a little more light-hearted got extra.

Because of how Brian was being treated, he had no reason to hold my hand and guide me, but he did. I spent most of my on-call nights with him, as our schedules seemed to mirror each other. There was one patient who was in a motorcycle accident, and he had four parallel lacerations on his arm that looked like what I imagined a mauling from a tiger would look like. Brian walked me through suturing the guy's arm. He was very helpful during my entire two weeks of trauma.

I got sick on my surgery rotation. I developed a cold like nothing I had ever experienced before. I probably had pneumonia, but I never went to see a doctor myself. Truthfully, I didn't tell people I was sick. I didn't want them to think I was looking for a way out of work. I took DayQuil around the clock, and every once in a while, I would change it up by taking Robitussin. I wanted to take NyQuil to help me sleep, but because I had to be at the hospital by six in the morning, I didn't want to oversleep. The DayQuil only lasted for four hours, so I would wake up in bad coughing fits every night. The surgery schedule drained me, but my illness was draining me even further.

Brian could detect my inward suffering, and although he was struggling himself, he never took his frustration out on me. I could tell he didn't appreciate the treatment he was getting, but he was still so nice to me, despite the attendings treating him like he was lower than dirt. One night, I coughed so badly, I felt like I had broken a rib. From then on, when I would take a deep breath, I would feel like someone stabbed me in my right side. Brian must have seen my pain. I yawned and the knife-like throb in my side made me shriek in torment, and I doubled over due to pain. I grabbed at my ribcage to prevent it from expanding any further and inflicting more discomfort. He asked me what happened, and I told him I was sick. He sent me to a call-room to get some sleep for the rest of the night, despite the amount of work that needed to be done. I'll never forget his kindness.

Once I was done with my two weeks of trauma, the rest of the surgery rotation wasn't so bad. I did two weeks of general surgery, and in doing so, I met two gastric bypass surgeons. They were both short guys with spunky attitudes, and they seemed to have Napoleon complexes. They weren't cruel to me, but they seemed insensitive to me in the way they treated patients who were under anesthesia. On some days of surgery, one of them would come in and approach the paralyzed patient and make some harsh statement like, "This one right here is a whopper!" referring to the size of the obese patients. He then would proceed to slap the patient on the abdomen as if he was slapping butts on a football field.

The first time I saw this, I was appalled. I kept wishing the patient would wake up from anesthesia and slap him in the face. Nickye threw a scalpel toward the surgeon out of anger. I would later learn this was harmless behavior compared to what some surgeons did in the operating room. I observed a surgeon throw things if their surgical techs did not hand them instruments in time. Some behavior I witnessed was mortifying and arrogant. If people knew how some surgeons act when the patients can't hear them, they would be appalled. I will say I developed a great appreciation for The Cranberries and Evanescence's music on this rotation. Dr. Porter, one of the bariatric surgeons, loved them and would play their music during operations. I was thankful for the music because it meant I wouldn't get quizzed. To this day, when I hear "Bring Me to Life," I instantly remember being in the cold operating room, watching surgical instruments get passed back and forth, as I shifted my weight between my legs so I could stay awake, despite my sleep-deprivation.

Most of my third and fourth-year rotations were good learning experiences, and I never felt like I was being singled out or picked on. However, in my fourth year, when I was doing some traveling rotations, I did an Emergency rotation in Orlando, Florida. The head of the department, Dr. Johnson, was not the nicest guy, and I don't know if it was just me he treated like crap or if he was an equal opportunity bully to students.

I was working one shift with him, and I knew he was the head of the department, so I was going to try to do everything I could to look like a rock star. I figured he had the most pull when it came to hiring residents. It only took one patient presentation to show me that no matter how hard I tried, I wasn't going to get into this particular residency program. The patient was a twenty-four-year-old male with a fever and a sore throat. I examined the patient but found it difficult to see the back of his throat because he could not open his mouth wide enough, and when I tried to use the tongue depressor to look at his tonsils, I still could not see very well. Despite that, I went back to present the case to Dr. Johnson.

We were sitting in the physicians' office, and I began. "Mr. Parks is a twenty-four-year-old male who has three days of fever and sore throat. He has no cough or cold symptoms, and he denies any difficulty breathing, but it hurts him to swallow. He thinks one of his co-workers may have had strep throat. He has been taking Tylenol and Motrin for fever and pain, but he stopped because it was too painful to swallow the pills. On physical exam, he is febrile, with a temperature of 101.5, and he is a little tachycardic, with a heart rate of 110. His blood pressure and oxygen are normal. His tonsils are swollen, and he does have exudate, but he has no lymphadenopathy. He has no heart murmurs, and his lungs are clear. He has good pulses and a benign abdominal exam. He also has no rash."

I felt proud of myself for just getting through the presentation because Dr. Johnson just stared at me the entire time without interrupting or asking any questions. He was quite intimidating in that fashion. I'm not sure if he made me nervous because I wanted to impress him so badly or if it was his oceanic blue eyes that lost no clarity behind his thick bifocals. "What's your diagnosis and plan?"

I swallowed the lump of anxiety stuck in my throat and responded, "I think he has strep throat, and I want to give him penicillin." I shivered, not because I was cold, although I always am in the hospital, but because he seemed to be staring straight through me. I have mesmerizing eyes of my own, so I typically am able to win staring contests, but his gaze made me look away. I felt like he was peeling back every layer of defense I had built up to that point, and just his look was enough to make me want to run and hide somewhere.

"Let me take a look at the patient." He got up and walked out. I had to get myself together because he had me shook; I felt like I had just watched a horror movie, and I hate horror movies. He seemed to have been gone forever, and when he came back, I saw a storm brewing in the ocean of his eyes, unlike anything I had seen before.

"Did you even examine the patient?"

Uh, oh. This isn't good. What did I do wrong? Did the patient say something bad about me? Why is he so mad? I'm going to flunk this rotation. Nickye put on a "dunce" hat and put herself in a corner in timeout. Despite all the negative thoughts in my head, I cleared my throat and tried to sound like I wasn't as terrified as I really was. "Yes, but it was difficult to see in the back of his throat because he had difficulty opening his mouth."

He snarled at me, "Did you not notice that one tonsil was pushing his uvula to the side? And you want to treat this man for strep throat. He has an abscess that needs to be drained. You would have sent this man home with his antibiotics, and then he would have come back a day later, likely in need of an operating room and a hospital admission!"

At that point, I was drowning in the storm in his eyes. I was at sea with no life jacket and there was no boat around to save me nor was there anything to help me float. Inside myself, I was panicking because my hopes of residency in Orlando died in the monsoon in this man's eyes. I finished that shift and never had the opportunity to redeem myself because I never got to work with Dr. Johnson again. With the different shifts of each attending, it was rare I got more than one opportunity to work alongside the same attending. Before I would return to my own hospital though, I did experience trauma like never before.

Years later, I can still recall the events. It was a typical shift in the ED: chest pains, abdominal pain, lacerations—but then, the medic radio went off. Static sounded, and then the sound of the ambulance sirens rang through. "This is medic fifty-one, we have a thirty-two-year-old male involved in a rollover motor vehicle collision. He had to be extracted by fire rescue, and we're bringing him in with a metal pole lodged in his back and leg..."

The nurse that answered the radio interrupted, "Did you say there's a pole lodged in his back and leg?"

"Affirmative," the medic responded. He continued, "We have fire rescue escorting us in. We aren't able to put him in C-spine immobilization because of the pole. They had to cut it but will likely need to cut it some more."

He gave more details, and once the report was finished, the nurse yelled out, "We're going to need trauma paged NOW!"

Suddenly, it appeared as if everyone that heard the report wanted to get a piece of this action. The attending I was working with that day looked at me and said, "This is real emergency medicine here. Go into the trauma bay with everyone else and pay close attention."

I thought this man would be yelling and screaming when he rolled in, but despite the fact there was a four-foot metal pole stabbing him in the back, continuing on out his right leg, he was awake and calm. The trauma doctor was in place, and he asked him, "Sir, do you hear me?"

The patient shook his head yes.

The trauma surgeon continued, "Can you feel any pain?"

He shook his head no.

I was watching with at least twenty-five other people; a crowd consisting of nurses, med students, residents, and attendings, and I was dumbfounded because not only was he awake, but he couldn't even feel the pain. The trauma doctors agreed they were not going to be able to remove the pole in the trauma bay, and they spoke with the firemen to formulate a plan as to how they were going to be able to get him into the operating room and remove the pole. I was fascinated, but I knew I was not going to get to see the end of this case, and sure enough, the trauma attending looked at all the extemporaneous people in the room and yelled out, "If you are not directly involved with this patient's care, you need to leave the room!"

We all looked at each other and reluctantly left the Trauma Bay. That's when I became more driven than ever. I reflected on that scenario and knew that Emergency Medicine was in my blood. That scene would have been enough to make an average person faint, but it thrilled me, and I wanted more. All I had to do was get into a program, but because I missed a peritonsillar abscess in front of the head of the emergency department, I knew I was going to have to find another place that would accept me.

MOMENT OF REFLECTION

There will be people in your life who make you question your own self-worth. These people can make it difficult for you to achieve certain goals. Are there ways you can keep others' negativity from making you feel hopeless? Formulate a plan now to prevent others' doubts from causing self-doubt. When I feel down because of other people I speak words of affirmation into my spirit, such as, "I am a child of God. God loves me. He cares about me. He will not give me more than I can handle." Write out your own words of affirmation, and use these as weapons against the enemy's attacks.

CHAPTER TWELVE

Praise Him in Advance

*Trust in the Lord with all thine heart; and lean not unto
thine own understanding. In all thy ways acknowledge him,
and he shall direct thy paths.*

Proverbs 3:5-6, KJV

The complete road to my career would be determined by the pick of my residency location. In order to get started in each specialty, medical students have to go through what's called Match Day. This is the day we find out if we have been chosen for a residency program and where we will be placed. It's the culmination of four long hard years of work and preparation. It's almost like picking a date for the prom.

You interview for a position wherever there's a program. I think of it like when you are getting to know someone. You sit down and question each other and see if you're the right fit for one another. Then comes the part where you wait to see if someone likes you, and, if chosen, your reward is the chance of a lifetime, to learn the tools necessary for your particular craft.

Here's the matching process. You rank the locations you interviewed, and they, in turn, rank the people they have interviewed. A computer program matches up the programs and the students based on the rankings. Once all the matching is done, if you end up on the list of a program, that is where you will be spending your next however many years of residency training. It's like Tinder without the swiping. Match Day is the actual day you find out where you are going. Most medical schools make a big deal out of it, and you invite your friends and family, and everyone sits in an auditorium, and they hand you an envelope determining your fate. Those that do not match get a notification a few days before, and then they have to "scramble."

Here's how the scramble process goes. Some programs don't get enough candidates to fill their residency slots. Some candidates don't get chosen by a residency program. The list of open slots is made known to those people that didn't match into a residency program, and they get to do the interview process all over again; hopefully, with better results. It's like what happens at the last minute when you don't get a prom date. You find out who is left, and you hopefully get a chance to find one person who will take pity on you and ask you out.

While I was in Orlando doing my emergency rotation, I was given the opportunity to interview so I wouldn't have to return at a different time at my expense. I had already received a chance to meet one of my interviewers when I worked with him, Dr. Johnson. I knew he wasn't going to choose me as a resident, but I was hoping my interview would at least make him think about it. I stepped into his office and shook his hand, hoping to start again brand new. He reached for my hand, and maybe it was just me, but I felt like he was trying to intimidate me from the start with the handshake. It seemed a little firmer than it needed to be, and in response, I tightened my grip in an attempt to prove I wasn't going to back down. He asked the typical interview questions politely, but at the end of the interview, as we were about to wrap up, he interjected with an almost sinister countenance, "Why should I choose you as a candidate for residency here?"

This could have been a question he asked every candidate, but because of our previous encounter in the ED, I knew he meant it a little more personally. He was basically telling me, "You aren't good enough, so you can forget me recommending you for a position." He didn't say that, but I felt it in his chilly gaze. The deep blue of his eyes seemed as forbidding as the iceberg that sank the Titanic. Up to that point, I almost felt like I had a chance, but then reality set in, and I was in the eighth grade again and realized I was not going to get the prom date of my dreams that year. I wasn't dating at the time and none of the really popular guys were available, so I ended up going by myself, which wasn't a big deal because it was only middle school, but it still hurt that nobody asked me to be their date. I really wanted to do residency in Orlando, but I knew it wasn't going to happen for me.

While trying to figure out what to say to Dr. Johnson, I felt my shoulders slump, and I almost reverted back to the insecure teenager I once was. Then, something came over me, and I straightened my posture, held my head up high, and retorted, "As a medical school student, I'm not expected to come here and know all of the answers. That's why I'm here, to learn and be taught by people in a position I want to be in one day. I'm not the smartest, but I'm determined and hard working. Whatever I attempt, I succeed in. If it's not here, it will be somewhere. But you can bet, someone is going to take a chance on me. I hope it's you." Nickye picked up a microphone and dropped it before walking off her invisible platform.

Dr. Johnson's face changed. I think I stunned him. We ended the interview and regardless of the outcome, I think I changed his perception of me.

My other interviews weren't as memorable. I interviewed at Duke University and my own residency program at ECU as well as at The University of Alabama at Birmingham (UAB). I felt comfortable at Duke. I felt like they liked me too. Because of that, I made them my top choice. I felt I had a chance to get in there, unlike how I felt about the program at Orlando. I felt comfortable at ECU also, but I hated the city of Greenville. There was nothing there but the school and hospital system, and it was an hour away from anywhere I really wanted to be. The program at UAB seemed cool but being a black girl in Alabama was going to be even more of a culture shock than ECU. So, my ranking order ended up being:

1. Duke
2. Orlando
3. ECU
4. UAB

The day we found out if we matched, I was nervous. I felt anxious all day like I was running a marathon while sitting still. My heart was racing, and I felt weak. I feared failure, and I was unsure anyone wanted me. When I found out I had indeed matched somewhere, I was relieved, but then an all-new sense of panic set in. Where was I going?

On Match Day, most of my classmates were in attendance, but I later found out we had a few who hadn't matched. I was just glad I wasn't one of them. We all filed in and sat in the first few rows of our auditorium. Both of my parents were in attendance, and as I was sitting waiting for my verdict. I turned around and looked nervously at them. I was the last one to get my envelope because with my last name being Worth, I was at the end of the lineup.

"Last, but not least, Kellye Worth."

I paused, took a deep breath, and walked up to the front to get my envelope. I waited to return to my seat before deciding if I was going to open now or wait until I was in the privacy of my own home. Others before me had mixed emotions. There were some who screamed in joy, some who smiled, but you couldn't tell what they were thinking, and then there were those with a look of horror on their faces. I prided myself on not letting anyone read my emotions, so I considered my options. Looking down at the envelope made my heart speed up even more, and I decided it was time to end the agony and find out my fate.

My hands began to shake. It seemed like it took hours to open the envelope because I suddenly felt like I had Parkinson's and couldn't stop the tremor. When I was finally able to pull out the sheet of paper with my life plan on it, I stared at it with mixed emotions. East Carolina University. I was numb. I just knew Duke had accepted me. I had already made plans in my mind, and I was ready to be in a place I knew since Durham was where I'd hung out sometimes as a teenager. It was also closer to A&T, so I would be able to make more frequent trips back to the school I loved.

As I was relinquishing the thoughts of happiness and familiarity, I didn't realize most everyone had gotten out of their seats and were going to greet their families. My parents were headed my way, and my mom instantly stopped smiling when she looked at my face. She knew what had happened before I said it. Don't get me wrong; I was happy I placed somewhere, and it was reassuring to know I would be in a place familiar to me, but I was so ready to leave Greenville; the thought I would be spending another three years in a place I no longer wanted to reside was disheartening.

Newton	Yolanda	St Lukes-Bethlehem-PA	Obstetrics-Gynecology
O'Malley	Patrick	Carolinas Med Ctr-NC	Emergency Medicine
Palmeri	Martin	Dartmouth-Hitchcock Med Ctr-NH	Internal Medicine-Primary
Pathan	Ayaz	Emory Univ SOM-GA	Emergency Medicine
Polen	Amy	Eastern VA Med School-VA	Pediatrics
Privette	Crystal	U Hlth Sys E Carolina-NC	Obstetrics-Gynecology
Rivera	Heather	Maine Medical Center	Medicine-Pediatrics
Ronan	David	U New Mexico SOM	Emergency Medicine
Simons	Christopher	University of Iowa Hospital & Clinics Program	Urology
Singh	Shinu	Boston U Med Ctr-MA	Internal Medicine
Snyder	Danal	U Hlth Sys E Carolina-NC	Medicine-Preliminary
Strickland	Julie	U Hlth Sys E Carolina-NC	Pediatrics
Tanner	John	University of Virginia	Family Practice
Tate	Matthew	Univ Louisville SOM-KY	Radiation Oncology
Tate	Matthew	Grand Rapids Med Ed-MI	Transitional
Taylor	William	University of Virginia	Internal Medicine
Turnbull	Jennifer	Moses H Cone Mem Hosp-NC	Family Practice
Valevich	Christina	U Hlth Sys E Carolina-NC	Pediatrics
Wait	Scott	Good Samaritan Reg Med Ctr-AZ	Surgery - Prelim / Neuro
Ward	Kimberly	U Alabama Hosp-Birmingham	Medicine-Pediatrics
Watson	Derek	U Hlth Sys E Carolina-NC	Phys Medicine & Rehab
Watson	Meredith	Orlando Reg Healthcare-FL	Obstetrics-Gynecology
Weiss	Anna	U Hlth Sys E Carolina-NC	Medicine-Pediatrics
Whetstone	David	University of Virginia	Emergency Medicine
Williams	Jonathan	U Hlth Sys E Carolina-NC	Emergency Medicine
Wittstein	Jocelyn	Duke Univ Med Ctr-NC	Orthopaedic Surgery
Worth	Kellye	U Hlth Sys E Carolina-NC	Emergency Medicine

MOMENT OF REFLECTION

I was ready to leave Greenville, but God had more for me there. If I'd had my way, I might have never met my husband, since we met my last year of residency. As you'll see in the next chapter, I didn't really come to be on fire for God until I became a member of Koinonia Christian Center, which also happened while I was in residency. What looked like punishment to me was actually a blessing in disguise. Look back over your life and think about situations God put you in or left you in when you didn't want to be there. Did you actually receive a blessing where you didn't see one? The next time you are upset because God doesn't give you what you asked for, remember the good that came out of it, so you'll begin to stop questioning why He does certain things.

CHAPTER THIRTEEN

Did You Know

[I always pray] that the God of our Lord Jesus Christ, the Father of glory, may grant you a spirit of wisdom and of revelation [that gives you a deep and personal and intimate insight] into the true knowledge of Him [for we know the Father through the Son]. And [I pray] that the eyes of your heart [the very center and core of your being] may be enlightened [flooded with light by the Holy Spirit], so that you will know and cherish the hope [the divine guarantee, the confident expectation] to which He has called you, the riches of His glorious inheritance in the saints (God's people), and [so that you will begin to know] what the immeasurable and unlimited and surpassing greatness of His [active, spiritual] power is in us who believe. These are in accordance with the working of His mighty strength

Ephesians 1:17-19, AMP

As I've stated, I always believed in God, and I was listening to His promptings even before I knew it was Him dropping hints. I didn't go to church often when I was growing up because I lived in a rural area with few choices. Although we lived in the country, my parents were from larger cities, and they were used to bigger churches. They didn't really like any of the churches in the area. Many were small and simplistic, relying on just traditional hymns and a piano or organ, without the full band and light show that can come with a larger and more technologically-focused church. As a baby Christian, I needed entertainment to keep me amused and attentive. Nothing is wrong with the condensed style of church, but it was hard to keep me focused. When we went to church as a family, we would go to my dad's home church, St. Paul AME (African Methodist Episcopal) in Raleigh, which was an hour away. It was just the right amount of everything. The choir was great, the congregation was just large enough, and the reverend gave a good 30-minute sermon that taught me something without boring me and taking forever.

Like a lot of kids, I didn't find church very interesting when I was younger. I remember going to one of my neighbor's churches. It was a black Baptist church, and all that meant to me is we would be in church half of the day. That was one reason my family didn't like going to those churches. None of us wanted to sit still that long. I got bored ten minutes after the message started most times. I think my mom was worse than I was. Because she had three young ladies to tend to, she seemed to pay less attention to the message than we did. Obviously, there weren't tablets to keep kids calm during that time, so my youngest sister Kourtnye would typically require a lot of attention. One particular Sunday at that church, the youth had to stand up and quote a scripture. I guess it was supposed to be a way for us to learn the Word, but at that time, I wasn't a Bible reader. There were probably only thirty to forty people in the church, but the thought of standing up in front of everyone was terrifying. My friend Tiffany must have known I didn't have a scripture prepared because she handed me a piece of paper with Psalm 23:1 written on it. I quickly memorized the verse.

When it was my turn, I stood up and murmured, "The Lord is my shepherd; I shall not want."

Shouts of "Amen," and "Hallelujah," were signs that I passed the unofficial test of holiness, so I smiled and quickly sat down before anyone had the chance to ask me for another verse.

I looked over at Tiffany and mouthed the words, "Thank you." I was so relieved. She nodded and then proceeded to quote her scripture. That experience kept me from ever wanting to go back to that church because I felt ashamed that I didn't know a Bible scripture. Luckily, we didn't go there many more times.

Because we lived an hour away from St. Paul, we didn't go to church regularly. Basically, we were Easter and Christmas Christians. We might throw in an extra service or two if there was a special occasion. I didn't really get serious in my walk with Christ until college. I was baptized there, and we joined as members after my grandfather died because it was his church, but I still didn't attend regularly.

I first became a member of my dad's church. Reverend Edmonds was great for me because he preached a good twenty to thirty minutes on one topic, and he didn't have us searching all over the Bible for scriptures. But he only gave me an introduction to Christ.

In college, most of the Christian students went to Mt. Zion Baptist

Church. It was a large church-much larger than my former church-and the Word was taught there a bit more. Because so many college students went there, it was actually kind of cool to attend service on Sundays because you could catch up with people. They also had a Bible study specifically for college students on Wednesday nights, at 9:00. Although I was getting more Word, it still wasn't until medical school that I became a regular church attendee.

When I first arrived at medical school, I knew it would take God, Jesus, and the Holy Spirit to get me through. Med school was no joke. That's why I knew it was important for me to join a church and attend regularly. Since I wasn't from Greenville and could be a bit of an introvert when out of my comfort zone, I didn't know a whole lot of people to ask about churches, and my classmates were new to the area as well. I went to about three different churches trying to feel comfortable. One was a holiness church. Now, I had only been to one holiness church before, and that was in college. I can't remember how I ended up there, but it was too much for me. I wasn't taught anything about speaking in tongues, and they were doing that, and then they had flag girls coming down the aisle. The only flag girls I knew of were in marching bands, so I did not like it and never went back.

When I got to the holiness church in Greenville, they were running around the church and speaking in tongues, and it scared me even more than the church I'd visited in college. I never went back there either. I'm not saying anything was wrong with that church, but because I wasn't taught the power of speaking in tongues, it was overwhelming. Growing up, the only time we stood was to read scripture and possibly if the praise and worship song was particularly moving. Other than that, we were seated and quiet.

Next, I went to a church called Koinonia Christian Center a couple of times. At the time, it was located in one of the more dangerous areas in Greenville. The first time I went was a Sunday service. The church wasn't that big in its initial location, so it was more like St. Paul for me, and I liked that. They only had a praise team, not a whole choir, which was new to me, and it turned me off a little. It was only because I was accustomed to a whole choir singing at the churches I would usually attend. Since I wasn't deep in the Word at that time and childlike when it came to being a Christian, I needed the whole choir with the band and all the bells and whistles so I could feel the Spirit. However, when the preacher got up to speak, I felt the Spirit awaken. Bishop Rosie O'neal had a strong presence and a booming voice, not one of those little tiny woman voices. I had never heard preaching like that before. I was impressed, so I went back to a Wednesday night Bible study. That's where I got deterred because, as I said before, it was in a rougher part of the city, and walking back to my car, parked on a dark road, after getting out of Bible study, didn't seem safe. After that second visit, I didn't go back.

I ended up at Cornerstone Baptist Church. I attended regularly, and once I found out I'd be staying in Greenville to do my residency, I figured I'd become a member of the church. The problem was, despite the fact I joined, it seemed impossible for me to get through the membership classes. There were only four, but I only made it through the first one. Being a resident, my time was limited, and my schedule was erratic, which meant I could never complete the classes in one session. I went to a second class, and there was only me and one other person who showed up that day, so they postponed the class. I was unaware that God had some other place for me to be; hence the reason I never made it through the entire cycle of the membership classes.

When I was in residency, a classmate invited me to a Women's Conference at—guess where—Koinonia Christian Center, otherwise known as KCC. This was four years after my initial visit. They had moved to a larger location in a different part of Greenville, which was a plus. Walking into the conference, I had no clue how moved I would be. It was November 9-12, 2005. I was on a rotation which allowed me to be available all three nights. God changed me those nights. There were three guest pastors and Bishop Rosie O'neal. The first night I attended, Dr. Claudette Freeman, co-founder of Seed Faith International Church, in Waldorf, Maryland, was the speaker. Her message was entitled, "Women Increasing Now," which was the title for the whole conference. She was preaching the Word, and she referenced so many scriptures I could not find them quickly enough. I wasn't too familiar with the order of the Bible at the time, but it didn't matter to me. After that night, I vowed I was going to get familiar with the Bible, so I could follow along better. I took notes, and I was scribbling furiously to absorb every inkling of knowledge I could. It was a great start to the conference, and because of it, I made plans to attend the next night.

The second night, Dr. Deloris Freeman, Pastor of Spirit of Faith Christian Center, in Temple Hills, Maryland, preached. She had a short, Toni Braxton-like haircut, her hair was dyed red like flames, and her personality was just as fiery. Her outfit spoke "expensive," and her shoes matched the same tone. Her topic was "Biblical Believing." She taught me that our beliefs determine our possibilities. I think that's when I first understood how much God wants us blessed. I knew it, but she reaffirmed what I already thought was true. That's when I figured out why I had been so successful up to that point. She stated, "There are four things that shape your belief system: your environment, repetitious information, what credible others have told you, and life experiences." Again, I rapidly scribbled down notes like I was preparing for a test. As I pondered her points, I silently thanked God for my family and role models who provided me with positive thoughts and positive experiences. By the time she was done, we were so filled with joy, she had us all in there screaming and crying. When she finished, I think we all felt like we could run the world, even before Beyoncé put it out there.

I returned the next night praying the next speaker and message were going to be as enriching as the last. Dr. Bridget Hilliard, co-founder of New Light Christian Center Church, in Houston, Texas, was the speaker. She, like Dr. Deloris Freeman, dressed like she was all business, and I admired her fashion sense. She was a bold preacher, and she was not afraid to declare it. I became infatuated with her confidence, and I instantly wished I had her way with words. Her message was on "Obtaining Favor." She spoke with alliteration so it would be easy to remember her message. It sounded so lyrical, I felt like she was performing spoken word. It was all I could do not to put my hands up and snap my fingers like I was in a coffee house. She said favor has to be Prepared for. You have to Petition for your favor. You must Pronounce it. You have to be Positioned for it. Finally, you have to Plant for it. In a nutshell, preparation was accepting Jesus as Savior, petition was prayer, pronouncing it was speaking and believing it, positioning was being in the proper environment, and planting was the act of putting a seed in the ground, such as serving others.

Because I had to work, I could not attend the final session where Bishop O'neal was the speaker. However, I had already seen her preach, so I was instantly sold that I would be attending church there regularly. After the Women's Conference, I never went back to Cornerstone. I now know I should have informed the church of my decision to leave, but suddenly I was "souled out" for Jesus in a way I'd never been before. Bishop O'neal is a Word preacher, and she taught me so much in the short time I was there. I was eagerly reading the Bible, and I soon joined the church. I even joined the greeter team. I just wanted to do all I could for and in the Kingdom of God.

KCC helped me to be a better Christian. I started understanding the Bible more and gained a closer relationship with God. It all became clear God was the reason I had been successful in certain areas, and I realized He had prompted me to do things early in life, such as going to A&T, deciding to be in the band at A&T, and applying to ECU for medical school. As I learned more about the Word, I developed a spirit of discernment which allowed me to see that some of the most important decisions I made in life were His design, and I hadn't even known it. At times, I felt such a strong urge to do things that didn't make sense to other people, but for some reason, I knew there was a certain path I was to follow. I'm now thankful for the early trials and the gentle nudging that He gave me. But I'm also thankful for the teachings that helped me understand how He was and always will continue to be the greatest presence in my life.

Greetings & Welcome,

We are so excited that you have decided to join us for Women's Conference! Prayer has gone forth that conference will be a life changing experience attendee. We pray that through this conference strengthened, refreshed, and infused with faith sincere hope that as a woman of God you will blessing promised to you to WIN in every area Through God and His supernatural power obstacle, situation, or circumstance that is God's glorious power. Through faith, we can remain victorious throughout life's journey.

1 John 5:4 states that "for whatsoever is overcometh the world; and this is the overcometh the world, even our faith." Wor will WIN when we submit to the lordship of J apply faith based upon the Word of God. through this conference you will be "Empo Infusion of Faith" to receive increase in your

May God continue to richly bless you!

Dr. Freeman is co-founder of the "Save the Seed" Ministry located in Waldorf, Maryland. She and her husband, Dr. Shine, oversee one of the largest 24 hour in-house deliverance ministries in the country and have done so for over 16 years. The revelation that God has given her has delivered thousands from drugs and alcohol abuse.

Dr. Freeman and her husband also have a world-wide television ministry through which they take their Deliverance Faith teaching of God's word to thousands of people across the country via daily and weekly TV broadcasts on the Word Network.

Dr. Deloris is the wife of Michael A. Freeman, Pastor and Founder of Spirit of Faith Christian Center. She assists her husband with a variety of duties to assure that his God-given mandate is carried out.

Dr. Deloris is the founder of Women Walking in The Word, a women's fellowship of over 1000 women that meet quarterly. She passionately encourages women to support and fulfill the purpose of God in their lives. Her teachings inspire and challenge women to develop a strong relationship with God and with their families. She is an anointed, uncompromising

Dr. Bridget is the wife of Dr. Ira Van Hilliard. She is the author of several books that have blessed the lives of thousands in the Body of Christ. Dr. Bridget is also the founder of "Women of the Word," and the "New Woman Attitude Ministries," with a television broadcast and monthly services.

Together, Drs. I.V. and Bridget E. Hilliard are the Co-Founders of New Light Christian Center Church, which has a membership of over 20,000 members. Their destiny is to build into God's people, PURPOSE, POWER, and PRAISE.

Bishop O'neal founded Koinonia Christian Center Church in 1989 with only seven members. Bishop O'neal's love and devotion to God and her family, along with her cheerful disposition and smile are the essence of her ministry and commitment to FEED, INSTRUCT, ORGANIZE, AND EQUIP the people of God. Ministries are continually being added to help serve the people in the surrounding communities, the state, the nation, and the world.

Bishop O'neal is the wife of Brother Toiriste O'neal. Together, they are committed to serving and leading KCC to the next level in ministry.

MOMENT OF REFLECTION

What does it mean to be on fire for God? Do you remember the first time you felt that way? Close your eyes and think back to that time. How did it feel? What did you do as a result of that feeling? Do you have that same passion for God or have life's daily activities/burdens drawn you away? If there are things in your life keeping you from desiring God like you used to, take this time to recommit your life to God, and allow Him to use you to do His work here on earth.

CHAPTER FOURTEEN

What They Gonna Do

Get rid of all bitterness, rage, and anger, brawling and slander,
along with every form of malice. Be kind and compassionate to one
another, forgiving each other, just as in Christ God forgave you.
Ephesians 4:31-32, NIV

Medical school was tough, but it didn't even begin to prepare me for what was next: my emergency medicine residency. I had been successful up to that point, so why wouldn't I get through the next hurdle? I always believed if I worked hard enough, I would eventually achieve my goal. There were multiple times in my three years of residency I didn't think I would make it. I had ambitious dreams. However, I didn't know some people would say or do things that would change my whole outlook on the career for which I had been preparing essentially my entire life.

The people who shaped my medical career, my attendings, had a significant role in my medical development. Attending physicians were the doctors in charge, the people who were supposed to teach me everything I would need to know about emergency medicine. There were three attending physicians in particular who almost made me doubt my purpose. Two of them were emergency medicine physicians, and one was a trauma surgeon.

Dr. House was a know-it-all New Yorker with a thick northern accent and a wise-guy attitude. He would quiz me on my patients and somehow make me feel like I was incompetent without saying one bad thing. I always felt like he just didn't like me, but then again, it might have simply been the Yankee in him, which offended me as a girl from the South.

Then there was Dr. Meyers. The only reason he didn't completely intimidate me was because he looked like a cartoon character to me. He had a thick mustache which seemed to have a life of its own when he spoke. Frequently disheveled hair sat on the top of his head, and he would ramble on and on so much I would often forget the original question he'd asked me. I think sometimes he would forget too.

I can still hear his voice in my head quizzing me. "Dr. Worth," he would say, while looking up at the ceiling, pondering a ridiculous question to ask. When he said the word doctor, I felt like it took minutes for him to get to the letter "r". The question would take even longer. "When you are intubating a patient..." dramatic pause while he crossed his arms and leaned against the nurses' station before resuming, "hooooow do you knooooow the tube has been placed correctly?"

By that point, Nickye had fallen asleep, waiting for him to finish asking the question. Dr. Meyers entertained me. He did unnerve me sometimes, as well, because he was always asking the most outlandish questions. However, it didn't seem like he was personally attacking me because he asked everyone eccentric questions. He was too smart for his own good.

The third physician was one I dreaded working with, the trauma surgeon, Dr. Schumacher. He literally terrified me. I'm so glad I wasn't trying to be a surgeon because I would have surely quit. He was an Army guy, and I think that in itself is half of the reason he seemed to me to be bipolar. He would be a gentle, calm soul one day and a mean-spirited drill sergeant the next. He maintained his military grooming, as he always wore a buzz cut and he rarely had facial hair, however, he didn't maintain his military figure. I always felt like he could use some bigger scrubs because they made him look like he had a beer-belly, and his pants never seemed to reach his ankles.

My trauma rotation was full of what I considered hazing. If fraternities and sororities get in trouble for it, residency programs should be punished as well. The sleep deprivation was unbelievable and dangerous. Multiple studies have shown that driving after being awake for over thirty hours is equivalent to driving while drunk. That's likely what prompted the eighty-hour workweek rule that went into effect while I was in residency. It was a national rule that residents could not work more than an average of eighty hours a week. However, because the rule said "average," we were still given unrealistic hours.

As an emergency medicine resident, I was required to complete a total of four months on trauma rotations throughout my three years of residency. Although this particular incident happened over a decade ago, I still have every detail seared into my mind. In my second year of residency, I was on my first of the two back-to-back months of trauma. It was a Saturday morning, and I was post-call, meaning I had been on call the previous day, and I had been at the hospital for twenty-eight hours up to that point. On the weekends, we didn't have a full staff, so the number of people able to witness my embarrassment was cut in half, thank God. We were slammed the night before, and I hadn't had a single minute of sleep. Needless to say, my mind was not fully functional. It was all I could do to muster up the strength to keep my eyelids pried open, let alone take care of patients.

We were in the trauma conference room, which normally holds thirty people, but there were only ten of us that day. I was presenting to a group comprised of Dr. Schumacher, as he was the attending on-call for the day, the attending who was on call with me the previous night, Dr. Smith; the on-call and post-call medical students, the on-call and post-call senior residents, the on-call junior resident, who would be taking my place for the day, the trauma fellow, and the nurse practitioner. We were sitting at conference tables which were set up in a square formation so everyone could see everyone else. As the junior resident, it was my responsibility to present the cases which had come in the previous night. We had one gentleman who presented to us with a gunshot wound. I began going over the details of how he had lost much blood in the field, and Dr. Schumacher stopped me to ask a question.

This is where the humiliation began. Here is another reason why I say residency is worse than pledging a fraternity or sorority. The physicians, who are supposed to be teaching you, are the "big brothers" or "big sisters," helping you go through the process of graduating to their level. You are supposed to do what your "big brothers or sisters" tell you to do, and if you make it through the initiation process, you'll become a member. There are always people trying to keep you from making it to the end because they feel you are weak, or they just like to get under your skin because it's fun for them. I'm not sure which category Dr. Schumacher fit, but it seemed like he didn't want me to make it to the end of the pledging process.

Dr. Schumacher asked, "Dr. Worth, explain to me the pathophysiology involved in hypovolemic shock."

Dr. Smith had gone over this a bit while we were taking care of the patient, so I began to answer his question. During this kind of presentation, when I answered one question correctly, a series of questions ensued, and the attending kept quizzing me until they either got to a question I couldn't answer or until they were impressed with my knowledge base. This is how they treated all the residents. As Dr. Schumacher kept asking questions, I knew he would not stop until he stumped me.

He asked me, "How does the renal system respond to hypovolemic shock?"

On any other day, I may have been able to answer the question, but I was so exhausted, it hurt to even form words. I was getting lightheaded, and I felt inebriated. I looked at Dr. Schumacher, as he seemed to realize he had me where he wanted me. I don't know if I imagined it, but I felt like a villainous smile was appearing on his face. The room was dead silent. I began looking around as all eighteen eyes were staring at me. I felt nauseated, and I didn't know what to say. You see, it was like a joke to some of the attendings. Once they figured out you didn't know the answer to their question, they were suddenly like a firing squad at a public execution.

When I hesitated to answer, he fired off another question. "Why did you have to call nephrology for a consult?"

I answered with a chuckle, "Because Dr. Smith asked me to." Nickye looked down and shook her head. This clearly wasn't the answer he wanted. I had to be delirious by answering that way. I knew Dr. Schumacher was not in any mood to joke, and I regretted the statement coming out of my mouth as soon as the words left my lips.

Looking back, Dr. Schumacher probably thought I was being sassy with him when in all actuality, I wasn't. He was trying to get me to think through the process of hypovolemia in renal failure, and I answered with the literal answer, which was I was doing what Dr. Smith told me to do. I wasn't even thinking, I was just trying to get through the morning.

Dr. Schumacher frowned; then, he gave me a tongue-lashing that I still have post-traumatic stress about today. He went into drill sergeant mode, as he began attacking me for wasting everyone's time. Each sentence he spoke from then on felt like bullets piercing my skin. I was looking at everyone staring at me, and I began to get tunnel vision. The last sentences I recalled went something like, "I know Dr. Smith went over this with you last night because he told me he did. Were you even paying attention? Why are we even teaching if you're not going to listen? Do you think this is a game? How are you going to take care of patients if you don't understand basic concepts? Now, we're going to go over this again since you clearly didn't get it. When a patient goes into hypovolemic shock…"

His words began trailing off in my mind, beginning to sound like the teacher in the Charlie Brown shows, "Wonk, wonk, wonk, wonk, wonk." I began to sweat, despite the room being ice-cold, and I felt like I was about to pass out. I couldn't breathe. I kept looking around the room, longing for someone to help me, to interject so he would stop. His yelling at me only lasted about five minutes, but it felt like five hours. I felt vomit creeping up in my throat, and I didn't know how I was going to ask him to please excuse me so I wouldn't vomit in front of everyone. Couldn't he understand I had been awake for thirty hours, for Heaven's sake? Nickye had already passed out, so she was no help to me at that point.

Though he was yelling at me, each word ricocheting off the walls, the only thing I actually heard was the clock on the wall in front of me, ticking away the seconds. The clock was so quiet, but its steady rhythm kept me calm, and suddenly, I could breathe. My vision came back into focus. His words started making sense again.

When he finally paused, before he reloaded his gun to fire at me some more, I got the nerve to say, "I'm too tired to understand what you are trying to teach me now. I promise I will read about hypovolemic shock when I've had some sleep."

I grimaced, expecting him to curse me out and inflict more torture on me. Nickye sat up and held up a white flag of surrender, hoping to end the scolding. Dr. Schumacher's face had the look of bewilderment, a mixture of surprise at my interjection and a hint of sympathy as if he partially understood I was operating on fumes and couldn't take much more. His whole countenance changed, and then he said, "Continue presenting the case."

Like that, it was over. Nickye sighed in relief. We went on to finish rounds, and I was able to go home for the day. From then on, I would never be the same. I vowed no one would ever make a fool out of me like that again. I could have quit, but I was not going to give him or people like him the satisfaction. His bullying gave me tough skin. Whoever said, "Words don't hurt," never had words rip through their heart in such a devastating manner. But, I didn't allow the situation to destroy me. The wounds Dr. Schumacher inflicted made me stronger. To this day, anytime someone raises their voice at me, I instantly get defensive, and I don't allow them to continue speaking to me disrespectfully. If they cannot voice their thoughts to me calmly, then the conversation will not resume. I don't let anyone talk down to me, all because of Dr. Schumacher. Maybe his treatment of me made me successful after all, but he also significantly scarred me.

I'll never forget another particular scenario in my second year. At the end of my first month on trauma, I was scheduled to be on call three calls in a row, meaning staying in the hospital overnight and not leaving until over thirty hours later, often staying awake working the entire thirty-plus hours. The six days basically went like this: I woke up at five o'clock in the morning to be at the hospital no later than six o'clock. I would see my patients and report for morning rounds by eight o'clock. I made sure to eat breakfast because I didn't know when the next meal was going to be. When on call, you had to admit any incoming traumas to the hospital, so the workload could increase at any time.

After morning rounds in the conference room, we physically rounded on all the patients on the service. That's when all ten to twenty people on the service would walk around to each patient's room and discuss the case and plan of care for the day. Once that was done, two to three hours later, you could eat lunch, if there were no incoming admissions. The afternoon was filled with performing procedures on patients and doing whatever tasks were assigned during morning rounds. Around three to four o'clock in the afternoon, the other residents would report out, and any remaining tasks were left to the on-call resident.

In the evenings and overnight, I would have a team made up of a senior resident, possibly a trauma fellow, maybe a medical student, and an attending physician, to take care of a service of anywhere from thirty to fifty patients. Most of the work fell to the junior resident, which meant sleep was rare. I was up all night, and I had to repeat the morning's activities, but I would get to go home after the morning conference or morning rounds, depending on which attending was running the show for the day, which was routinely around ten to eleven o'clock the next morning. Every call was the potential to be awake and in the hospital for around thirty hours, give or take an hour. After call, I would go home, eat, shower, get in the bed, wake up some time in the afternoon to eat dinner, watch TV or study for a couple of hours, go back to sleep, and then repeat the same cycle the next day. That went on for six days.

When I got the schedule for my first month and saw this was what the end of my first month of trauma was going to look like, I was beyond outraged. But there was nothing I could do about it. In six days, I was going to work ninety hours, thirty of them in one shift. What I didn't know was it would get worse. After my second call in a row, I got my schedule for the next month of trauma. I was exhausted because I had not slept the entire night. We were in the conference room, and I was getting ready to go home, while the rest of the team was going to do hospital rounds. The senior resident handed me my schedule, and without a word, quickly exited the conference room. I looked down at my life timetable for the next month. I was on call for another two calls in a row. In total, I ended up on call for five calls in a row, meaning, in a matter of ten days, I would work one hundred fifty hours. Most people would work that many hours in a month; I would do it in less than two weeks. Tears welled up in my eyes. I sat down and immediately started crying. I wasn't ordinarily a crier. I preferred to use anger as my choice emotion when things weren't going my way. Even Nickye was on the verge of tears. It was like a dam burst, and all my emotions spilled out of my eyes. I'm glad I was alone because I didn't want anyone else to see my weakness, but fatigue trumped my desire to put on a brave face.

There was a third episode which stands out in my mind as horrific. This time I was on my internal medicine rotation and in my second year of residency. I was on call yet again. It seemed that being on call was when I would make mistakes. Fatigue and medicine don't mix, but who am I to make any changes to the system? I had a seventy-something-year-old female being admitted for pneumonia and sepsis. She was awake and talking to me when she was first admitted to the hospital. She became sicker. My senior resident was actually the same year as me, but a medicine resident, therefore, outranking me. Our relationship was amicable, and we had worked together before. She instructed me to put in a central line on the patient. She knew I had no problem with performing this, so she left me to do it on my own while she tended to some other patients.

The patient was nice, and her family was kind as well. I knew putting the central line in would hurt, so I didn't want to, but it had to be done. I was in her hospital room all gowned up in my overly large blue sterile gown, my hair hidden beneath a blue paper bonnet. The gown helped to keep me warm in the chilly room. The patient was awake, but her health was rapidly declining as I was performing the procedure. At that time, we were performing a lot of central lines in the femoral artery near the groin, and if I hadn't been in a rush, I would have reviewed her chart more thoroughly and decided to do a subclavian central line in the chest. However, I had another patient in the ED being admitted who was going to require a history and physical exam, and I wanted to get in a power nap at some time that night. I was wiping down the patient's leg with betadine and numbing her up with lidocaine. I inserted the needle and got blood in the syringe, and I knew I was in the right place, but as I tried to insert a wire in the vein so I could then insert a catheter, the wire got stuck. I tried to dislodge it but had to pull really hard to get it loose. She ended up with a large hematoma as a result of my forceful tugging. I then moved to the other leg, where I got the central line in. I took off my protective gear, discarded all my needles and sharp items, and got moving to my next task.

The next morning, someone else evaluated the elderly pneumonia patient because I was assigned to a different floor, so I didn't realize the hematoma in her groin had become significantly larger. When we went on floor rounds and evaluated each patient as a team, the attending, who I wasn't really fond of, began criticizing my work.

"Who put in this central line?"

Not sure why he was asking, I slowly responded, "It was me."

"Why would you perform a femoral line on a patient who had a femoral-popliteal bypass?"

In simple terms, a femoral-popliteal bypass is done to get around a blockage in the blood vessel using a piece of another blood vessel. Because she had that procedure, it hadn't been a good idea to put a central line in that vessel because it could close off the newly opened vessel.

The patient had worsened overnight, unbeknownst to me, since I was handling all of the new admissions from the emergency department. Instantly, I froze, wondering if I had caused her condition to deteriorate with my botched-up attempt to place the femoral line. Later, I would learn the pneumonia had worsened, but it wasn't my fault. At the time, though, a rush of guilt overcame me. This was the first time I'd felt like I had compromised a patient's care, and I began to tremble due to fear.

My attending was waiting for an answer, and I never gave him one. Nickye turned away with her hands held up in the air in surrender, as if to say it wasn't her fault I messed up. My attending looked back at the patient's leg, and the third-year resident on my service asked me to go get the chart which was outside the room. My legs felt like I was a toddler just beginning to walk, and my head felt as heavy as a watermelon. I approached the nurse's station to ask for the chart, but just before I could reach it, my legs buckled, and I began to pass out. A male nurse must have seen me stumbling, so he caught me before I hit the floor. I didn't actually lose consciousness. I wanted to, though, because I was ashamed. I don't usually show any signs of weakness, even when I'm being humiliated, so I don't know if it was a combination of fatigue and embarrassment, but for the first time in my life, I almost passed out. The third-year resident came over to me and helped me up, but as I was getting back on my feet, I could feel vomit about to erupt like lava. I began stumbling to the restroom, and she came with me. I made it just in time. She asked, "Are you okay?" with genuine concern in her voice.

I lied and said, "I've been sick all night. I didn't want to tell anyone." I didn't want to look like a punk, hence the lie. I surmised they would have sympathy for me if they'd thought I had been sick all night and toughed it out for the good of patient care.

She went back to the attending and told him I needed to be excused from rounds. He reluctantly agreed, and I received permission to go home early after being at the hospital for over thirty hours with maybe a one-hour nap. I instantly went to bed to try to forget the shame which had occurred that day. When I returned the next day, the patient with pneumonia had died. I blamed myself, though it wasn't my fault. It took me months to get over that moment and the patient's death.

Despite the horrific attendings who have come my way, there were some who were actually complimentary to me and helped me through the world of the critical white men who seemed to be the ones who had it in for me. One lady, in particular, was a spicy Latina woman, Dr. Amelia Lopez. Everyone loved Dr. Lopez. She was married to the sweetest and most soft-spoken giant, Dr. John Mitchell, who was also an emergency medicine attending. Dr. Mitchell approached seven feet, but he was not quite there, and one would think he would speak with a booming voice to match his size, but I often had to get close to him to hear him. The two of them seemed to be opposites, seeing as she was petite and boisterous, and he was tall and quiet. It was laughable to see the two of them together, but they complimented each other perfectly.

Dr. Lopez was an awesome teacher. She was funny, and she didn't try to make you feel dumb if you didn't know the answer to every question she asked. In fact, it was almost like she didn't want you to know the answer because it would give her the opportunity to teach it to you, and not in a condescending fashion. I liked it when I got to work with Dr. Lopez. She would dart in and out of the patients' rooms with such style and grace. I often viewed her movements as salsa-like. It was a party working with her. I would say I pattern my current practice after her, thinking about it now. I bounce in and out of rooms with a rhythm of my own. It's like a choreographed music video.

Despite Dr. Lopez being so fun to work with, if you upset her, the lady could quickly put you in your place. We had a patient we worked on together who ended up with unforeseeable complications, and she wanted me to present the case in our morbidity and mortality rounds. I was never a public speaker, and this was going to be in front of both the internal medicine residents and the emergency residents in our hospital auditorium. I initially reluctantly agreed, but about one week before the presentation, I realized the morning conference was going to be the day after I worked a night shift. I knew I was not going to be able to stay awake long enough to present, let alone string together words that would actually make sense to an audience of at least fifty people.

I'll never forget the look she gave me. She couldn't have been much taller than five feet, and I had at least five inches on her, but I felt one-foot tall after she scolded me. "Don't you ever agree to do something for me, then back out at the last minute."

She didn't yell, curse, or demean me in any way. However, I felt like I let her down. Nickye slouched down, put up her index finger as a gesture similar to raising her hand, also known as the church finger, and excused herself from the room in shame. I was upset at myself, despite the fact I didn't feel like I was wrong for changing my mind. When she initially inquired whether or not I would present the case, she stated if I didn't want to do it, the internal medicine resident could do it, as the patient was admitted to their service. I knew someone else could discuss the patient's care, and I had given her a week's notice. However, Dr. Lopez was one of those people you didn't want to disappoint, not because of the repercussions, but because you wanted her to be proud of you. Fortunately, she didn't seem to hold that day against me, and so it continued to be a joy to work with her.

Another of the emergency attendings I liked to work with was Dr. Schumacher, the female version. Yes; you guessed it, related to male Schumacher—ex-wife to be exact. They say opposites attract, but I can't even begin to understand how the two of them ended up married. Although I never learned the details, it was no surprise to me they divorced. I didn't see them interact much, so if Dr. Schumacher hadn't kept her husband's last name, I would have never known. She, like Dr. Lopez, was easy to work with. Although she seemed to have blonde moments that matched her blonde hair, she was very knowledgeable and didn't try to intimidate me.

At one point, she became the residency director. I was still having trouble with standardized exams, and so once again, I had to meet outside of normal work hours to study with her and a few other students who needed a little extra help. Once again, I was told I needed help, and once again, I felt like I wasn't supposed to need help. Insert angry black woman again, although I was not quite as bad as I was at the beginning with Virginia. Dr. Schumacher was like those cheerleaders on television who were just so positive and so perky you wanted to slap them sometimes. I did like her though. "You guys can do this! It's all about finding out what your weakness is." Nickye picked up Dr. Schumacher's pom-pom and threw it in her face.

Black women don't have weaknesses, not ones we'll admit to, anyway. Malcolm X once said, "The most disrespected person in America is the black woman. The most unprotected person in America is the black woman. The most neglected person in America is the black woman." While I do not necessarily agree with the rest of his speech or his "by any means necessary" theology, for many of us, those statements hold true. As such, we are taught to grin and bear it. We expect the weight of the world to fall on our shoulders, and we're supposed to overcome by any means necessary, all the while, letting no one see us struggle. Medical school had already shown me my weaknesses, and I got a second chance in residency to take the weakness test again. The truth is, it's okay to show weakness sometimes—2 Corinthians 12:10 proves where we are weak, He is strong. I learned leaning on others is acceptable, and revealing those weak areas allows Christ to work in me.

Dr. Schumacher's overly obnoxious positivity made me hate going to the scheduled study groups. I didn't want to sit around a table strategizing on how not to be a failure. Notwithstanding the reality that once again, I felt like a remedial student, Dr. Schumacher kept pushing me to succeed. I needed people like her, and I'm glad she was there.

MOMENT OF REFLECTION

My attendings shaped my career, whether in a good way or a bad way. In my current practice, I sometimes have the opportunity to work with residents. I let college students shadow me as well. I treat residents and college students the same, realizing I have the ability to make a good or bad impression on them. Because I did not care for some of the treatment I received, I try to make the experience positive for the students I work with. I do the same for my nurses and other ancillary staff. No matter what their level, I treat everyone that falls under my leadership with respect. If you are a leader, how do you treat those you lead? If you are not a leader, is there someone who has a leadership role over you? Do they treat you with respect? Think about instances where you have been the leader and when you have been the one under someone's leadership. What can you learn about the way you should treat people in either situation?

CHAPTER FIFTEEN

One Sweet Day

Blessed are they that mourn: for they shall be comforted.
Matthew 5:4, KJV

Death is not what we typically think about in medicine. Early in our career as doctors, we think about all the lives we will save, but we don't think about the ones beyond our help. We aren't God—we don't have the capacity to raise anyone from the dead, nor should we. In medical school, we had simulated patient encounters, and one of the teaching situations was how to tell family members about death. Our instructors taught us to clearly say the word "died" and not to use phrases like, "no longer here" or "passed." When dealing with death, family members may not understand if we use other terms to describe death. They taught us that if you said to a family member, "Your loved one is no longer with us," the family member might think they had been transferred to another hospital or something and assume their body was no longer physically on the premises, not that they died.

My patient simulation experience was nothing like the real thing. Our patient simulation station was typically in a large trailer with four or five rooms, just outside the medical school. We went in a few at a time, and I was handed a chart by one of the instructors, as I stood outside a door leading to my simulated patient. I read through the make-believe scenario I was given. I had the wife of an eighty-year-old man who had died of cardiac arrest. The patient was brought in by medics, and CPR was performed for ten minutes, but a pulse was never obtained. I had to explain this to the wife. Once we were given the approval to step into the room, I knocked on the door.

"Come in," uttered the mock wife.

I entered slowly, trying to make the situation seem as real as possible. We were evaluated on these encounters, so I always put as much effort as I could into it. However, it never really felt realistic to me, and it seemed more like I was auditioning for a role on the show ER. Seated in a chair against the back wall of the room was an elderly woman who smiled when she saw me. I extended my hand out to the wife as I entered the room.

"Hello, I'm Dr. Worth." I shook the wife's hand and proceeded to pull up the stool that was across the room. I knew for sure the stool was positioned as far away as possible for a reason. We were taught to try to be as accommodating as we could be to patients by sitting down and not standing over them to display authority.

"How's my husband, Dr. Worth? When will I be able to see him?" The look of concern on the lady's face was almost genuine. The people in these encounters were paid actors, and some were better than others. The more realistic the actor, the better I was able to get in character.

"You will be able to see him soon, but I needed to talk with you first. When your husband came in, the paramedics were performing CPR. We gave him medicine to try to restart his heart, but we were unable to, and he has died." End scene. Job well done. Now, let's wrap this situation up and carry on with the day. Nickye patted herself on the back, applied her robe, and proceeded to her dressing room.

The wife shook her head from side to side and took off her eyeglasses. "George was supposed to help me clean the garage this weekend. What am I supposed to do now?" The lady looked like she was about to cry, and her eyes watered.

Clearly, the scenario was not over. What now? Nickye stopped in her tracks, rolled her eyes, took off her robe, and reluctantly got back into character. I looked around trying to figure out what to do next. There was a table in the corner of the room with a box of tissues on it. I got up and handed the lady the tissue box while I got back into character. "Is there anyone I can call to come to the hospital with you?"

"Well, there's my son, but it will take him hours to get here," she wiped at her eyes, although no actual tears had fallen.

"Would you like for us to call him for you?"

"Yes, but I need to see George now."

I wasn't sure how far the scenario was going to go, so I just kept at it. "Well, how about we have one of the nurses call your son while I take you in to see George. I will also call the chaplain so you can have someone to sit with you if you'd like."

The wife nodded in approval, and then her face went from sad and withdrawn to upbeat and warm. Apparently, I did what I was supposed to. She gave me feedback on my approach, and it appeared to have been a job well done.

During my residency, when I first needed to talk to a family about death, the scenario was nothing like what I had practiced. My attending physician did all of the talking while I was an onlooker. A fifty-something-year-old black woman was the patient, and she had numerous medical problems, including high blood pressure and diabetes. She was brought in by paramedics in full arrest, and we took over CPR when she arrived. We were unable to resuscitate her. My attending, Dr. Hicks, instructed me to come with him to deliver the news to the family. We walked down the hall to the family conference room.

I was unprepared as we arrived at the door of the family conference room. There were about twelve people of various ages crammed in a room which only had seating for half as many. Thank God Dr. Hicks was going to deliver the bad news. My patient simulation clearly did not prepare me for this. Dr. Hicks began, "Hey, I'm Dr. Hicks. How are you all related to Mrs. Williams?"

An older gentleman seated on the couch with two younger ladies answered, "I'm her husband. These are her two daughters, and standing by the door, is her son. Her sisters and some friends are here also."

Dr. Hicks extended his hand out to the eldest, Mr. Williams. I was standing up against the door close to her son. There was nowhere for Dr. Hicks or me to sit, and no one got up to offer a seat, so we stood along with the other family members without seats. Dr. Hicks continued, "I just wanted to let you all know the paramedics gave the best care they could, and once Mrs. Williams arrived, we took over CPR. We gave her medications to try to get her heart pumping on its own, but the medicines were not effective. We did everything we could, but her heart never restarted, and unfortunately, she has died."

I figured there would be tears and screams because black families can be pretty expressive, sometimes overly so. As I looked around the room at the friends and family processing the news of their loved one's death, a medium-sized metal trash can whizzed past my face. I dodged it and stepped out of the room. The son picked the trash can up again and was about to throw it when another family member grabbed his hands and instructed him to put it down. He rushed out of the room crying and screaming, "No, no, no," while the family member who saved the trash can from being hurtled down the hall went with him. The two daughters started wailing like banshees, and the husband just held his face in his hands. Other friends and family started hugging them and each other while also screaming out in chorus. I looked at Dr. Hicks, who looked as uncomfortable as I did. I was worried it was all too much for him too, but as a nurse came down the hall to help us, he began to speak up again.

"I want to let you all back to see her, but we want to get her cleaned up. The nurse will come and get you once we have prepared the room, and you all will be able to visit with her. I will be around to answer any questions you may have. I'm sorry for your loss."

Nobody seemed to be paying much attention at this point, as they were all hugged up in groups trying to console each other. Dr. Hicks interjected, "We'll be back to get you." He stepped out of the room, and as we were walking back to the Emergency Department, he looked at me with concern. "Are you okay?"

"Besides having to dodge a flying trash receptacle, I'm as good as can be expected, I guess."

Dr. Hicks chuckled a little, "I thought they were going to start breaking things!"

"I did too. I'm afraid of what's going to happen when they go in the room to see her."

Dr. Hicks stopped abruptly. "You're right. Maybe we should have security nearby."

We both laughed, and that was that. I was a second-year resident at that time, and despite the fact the whole situation was sorrowful, I still had other patients to care for that shift. By this point in my career, I had emotions of steel. It didn't take long to stop thinking of people as human beings. People became obstacles to finishing tasks and barriers to power naps when on call.

While I was on my internal medicine rotation, we had patients on the fine line between death and the afterlife. As doctors, we knew they had no quality of life, but family members were hesitant to stop all life-saving measures. It seems cruel a doctor would be telling family members to stop allowing medicine to keep their loved ones alive, but sometimes, it was our job.

I remember one family in particular. When there are critical decisions families need to make, we have family conferences. This is when the medical team meets with key decision-makers in a patient's family to create a plan of care and a course of treatment. In this instance, the patient was a seventy-five-year-old female in a vegetative state, as a result of a massive stroke. She was on my team's service for over three weeks, and she never showed any signs of improvement or life. As a treatment team, we knew the likelihood of any brain activity was essentially zero, so once we determined it was a futile use of resources to continue keeping this patient alive, we had the task of making the family understand so we could withdraw care. Although it is harsh to consider "resources" over someone's life, residency and the demands of being a doctor make many of us robotic. We learn we are never supposed to make mistakes, and we can't allow ourselves to feel emotions because there's always another patient in need of care. Many patients expect us to work through hunger, fatigue, and sadness, not considering the fact we have needs also. At some point, I and countless other physicians seem to stop thinking of patients and family members as people.

Every day, for one week at morning rounds, when I presented this patient to the team, my report was the same. "Mrs. Jones is our seventy-five-year-old African-American female who presented due to a stroke. This is hospital day twenty-four. Overnight she has maintained on the ventilator without complications. On physical exam, she continues to be unresponsive to any stimuli, verbal or painful. She continues to be on tube feeds, and her labs have been stable. Her prognosis continues to be poor. Nursing staff tells me the family is ready to discuss options."

My attending, Dr. Marks looked unenthused. "Is it going to be more of the same or are they ready to face reality?" We had spoken to the family a number of times, and despite our best efforts, they weren't ready to give up on a miracle. Don't get me wrong. As a Christian, I believe in unexplainable healings, but at some point, one has to decide, is it faith in God that keeps you holding on for a miracle or selfishness for wanting to keep a family member on life support, when a poor quality of life is the likely outcome? Sometimes, people's time here on earth is done, and God's will determines the outcome.

"I don't know. They weren't available this morning to speak with."

We consulted the nurse, Becky, who located the family and set up a time for us to meet with them. Once we confirmed the time for our family conference, we ate lunch, and Dr. Marks dismissed the group, with the exception of me and the senior resident on our service. "Alright ladies, let's see where this conference is going."

Walking from the cafeteria to the ICU, Dr. Marks and my senior resident Laura were happily engaged in conversation, while I was lingering in the background, looking over the list of tasks to complete for the afternoon. I was on call that night, so I couldn't help but think how awesome it would be if we could withdraw care for Mrs. Jones, so there would be one less person to round on the next morning. I know it sounds cruel, but as I said, residency turns you into a different person. Somewhere in the mix of trying to learn all the clinical information you can, so you can heal the world, you realize some of your patients are going to die, and there is nothing you can do to stop it. When on call, you hope you can arrange for death to be early in your afternoon so you can finish the rest of your tasks for the night and have time to eat dinner before the evening admissions begin.

Realizing I wasn't keeping up with my team, I lengthened my strides and increased my pace. Laura and Dr. Marks hadn't realized I was lagging behind. By the time we reached the ICU floor, Laura and Dr. Marks stopped joking and put on serious doctor faces. I already had on my somber doctor face because I was fearing this conversation wasn't going to go our way, and I was going to continue to have Mrs. Jones as one of the many patients on my list. Becky was looking through Mrs. Jones' chart when we walked up. She slammed the chart closed and stood up. "They're all here waiting for you guys."

With Becky joining the group, the four of us walked into the family conference room. It was a small room with a rectangular table in the middle. Already seated were Mrs. Jones' brother and sister, along with her two daughters and son. She wasn't married, so there was no spouse. They were all seated on one side of the table. My team pulled out chairs to sit across from them while Dr. Marks reached out his hand to shake hands with each of the family members before he sat down. The screech of his chair being pulled out from under the table made me cringe. It seemed so loud in contrast to the quiet in the room.

Dr. Marks opened up. "I understand you all wanted to meet and talk about options for Mrs. Jones' further treatment?"

Mrs. Jones' eldest daughter, who was the designated power of attorney, spoke up. "We know y'all been telling us things don't look good. Has anything changed?"

I was glad Dr. Marks was leading this conversation because, as a second-year resident, I still was not comfortable explaining things to patients or family when it came to bad news. "I'm afraid not. At this point, you as the people that know her best have to think, would she want to live like this?"

Her son quickly interjected, "If we want to keep her alive, is there anything else we can do? Are there medications we can give her?"

Come on, man! The conversation was not going in my favor. While maintaining my serious, engaged expression, Nickye was pouting. Guess I won't be crossing her name off the list tonight. Once again, pre-residency, I would never have had thoughts like that, but sleep deprivation and an overflowing workload made me harsh and hard-hearted.

To interrupt my horrible thoughts, Dr. Marks explained, "There's nothing more we are doing. At some point soon, we are going to have to discuss moving her to a rehabilitation facility. We can't keep her here, as we are no longer performing any active treatments. At this point, we are just keeping her breathing with the ventilator. She has not shown any brain activity, and there are no interventions we can do to change this."

As I looked at the dejection on each of Mrs. Jones' loved ones' faces, the sadness was evident, but all I could think about was the transfer papers I would have to fill out in order to transfer her to a rehab facility. Great! Let's get ready to add that to the growing to-do-list already overwhelming my mind. Nickye was preparing a pot of coffee in anticipation of a long night.

Mrs. Jones' brother then spoke up. "Y'all been crying over this for the past week. She ain't coming back. We gotta move on. She wouldn't want this!"

Hold up! There was hope. At least somebody had stepped out of Neverland, where the patient was never going to be off my service. I tried not to look hopeful, but the possibility of a power nap on the night's call was looking more realistic. Nickye stopped brewing the coffee.

The youngest daughter surprised me by looking over at me, interrupting my brief moment of hope. "If this was your mom, what would you do?"

Oh no! At that moment, she wanted me to speak. Nickye turned around as if to say, "Who? Me?" The daughter and I had a bit of a rapport because I had spoken with her a couple of times to give her updates on her mother's care. I don't know if she was looking to me because I was the only black person in the room or because I might have unknowingly formed some small bond with her. I wasn't sure if I should answer, and I definitely didn't want to say the wrong thing. I looked over at Dr. Marks, and he nodded his approval. Great! Thanks for saving me, Dr. Marks. Way to be a leader.

I paused for what was only seconds, but to me, it felt like minutes. I opened my mouth, then closed it. I was going to say some scholarly doctor thing, but I put myself in her shoes. I was the oldest of my siblings, so if something were to happen to my mom, I would be the one everybody looked to for a definitive decision. With that thought in mind, I cleared my throat before giving my advice.

"I, uh, I can't tell you what to do, but…" Dr. Marks was expressionless, so I continued. "My mom can't sit still. I get that from her. I have been taking care of your mom for a few weeks, and she hasn't improved. I wouldn't want to be trapped in a bed letting a machine breathe for me if I'm almost certainly not going to get better, and I wouldn't want that for my mom, either."

She started crying, which made everyone else in the family start crying. Briefly, I felt the weight of their decision, but then my pager vibrated, and I quickly jumped back into my doctor character. My empathy turned off just as quickly as my pager received a message. All I could think was, *who wants me to do something now?*

Mrs. Jones' brother asked, "Can we have time to talk alone?"

Dr. Marks slid back his chair, once again loudly, which again interrupted the silence in the room. "We'll step outside. Poke your head out when you're ready."

My team exited, and I walked over to a phone to answer the page. One of the other residents was ready to check out with me and give me any updates or need-to-knows on their patients. By the time the resident met me in the ICU and told me what I needed to do for his patients, Mrs. Jones' daughter stepped out of the conference room.

"We're ready."

My team filed back into the conference room and once again sat down with eager anticipation.

In between tears, Mrs. Jones' daughter blurted, "Take her off!" She moaned in pain, and momentarily, my heart ached for her, but I, truthfully, was relieved.

Dr. Marks sat up in his chair. "I have to clarify. You want us to stop all life-saving measures?"

Mrs. Jones' daughter nodded, not looking up.

Dr. Marks patiently responded, "You have to say yes."

She wiped a tear away, looked up, and muttered, "Yes."

On the one hand, I was thrilled I would have one less patient to round on the next morning, but then I looked at the daughter, and I found emotion again. This lady was going to have to learn to live without her mother, and I was celebrating the fact I would possibly have less work to do in the morning.

That was the constant battle I had during residency. Because we were overworked and underpaid, it became easy to suppress emotion. I didn't have time for it. I sometimes feel like a part of me died during residency. I went into the field thinking I was going to heal the world, and everyone would appreciate me for it. The reality was different, and I became jaded as a result. If there were only one thing I could change about my time during residency, it would be that I not let the stress change who I was as a person. I allowed myself to let go of human emotion in order to survive, and while it allowed me to function as a doctor, it didn't allow me to be the caring person I'd always been. I am glad to say that later in life, I did find that person again, and she is not dead after all.

Life's burdens and struggles can sometimes change your outlook on life, whether you're in the medical field or just experiencing life in general. You can become hard-hearted and a shell of your former self. It is important to stay rooted in the Word of God or do whatever you can to be able to maintain kindness in adversity. It took me years to understand I didn't have to let stress change who I am or how I act. I now use prayer and scripture to keep me at peace, even when the world is full of chaos. I urge you to do the same.

MOMENT OF REFLECTION

With life comes death. Sometimes it happens too early or tragically. For those working in healthcare, it can be difficult to deal with patients dying. A new nurse once asked if she would ever get over losing patients. My answer was to try to focus not on death but on the family members who are left behind. When having to give people news of a loved one's death, be aware they can remember that moment for a lifetime. Your duty as a healthcare worker should be to show love and kindness to the family and bless them with empathy as they say their goodbyes. A genuine hug or a small prayer with them could make all the difference. You could be the very one who makes the death a little more bearable. Life is stressful in a plethora of occupations and in general everyday living. The same rules apply. You don't know what issues other people have in their personal lives. Show kindness towards others, even when they are being difficult to deal with. It can be unbelievable what a kind word can do for someone, and it may even change their actions toward you.

CHAPTER SIXTEEN

God's Plan

For God so loved the world that he gave his one and only Son,
that whoever believes in him shall not perish but have eternal life.

John 3:16, NIV

Throughout my journey to becoming a practicing physician, I never had the time to just sit and reflect on my journey in life up to and throughout residency. I had no idea things I experienced and the lessons I'd learned could benefit others. As I matured in Christ, I began to understand one of my spiritual gifts is exhortation. An exhorter is one who strongly encourages someone to do something. While I am not one to force anything on anyone, I do have a way of making people believe they can accomplish goals that may seem insurmountable. Meeting Kedeja was one of the most rewarding experiences, and I'm so thankful God brought her to me. She told me I literally changed her life. The truth of the matter is, she did the same for me.

At the point in my life when I met Kedeja, I was beginning to feel the burnout of practicing emergency medicine. I was stressed to the point of wanting to get out of medicine completely. I had inquired of God many times why I had prepared my entire life for a career that was beating me down and destroying me physically, spiritually, and emotionally. I wondered why He allowed me to feel trapped in a lifestyle I knew was unlikely to change. I thought that because it was God's plan for my life to be a physician, I was just going to have to take up my cross and bear it.

When I saw how my words turned Kedeja into a more confident and self-assured young woman, I knew my purpose was greater than just being a doctor. She was the first of many mentees to come. I have seven young ladies who I currently mentor, six being students at A&T and Kedeja being my medical student mentee. The impact I have made on their lives is what keeps me going when I'm feeling burned out with medicine. After seeing my influence on their lives, I wanted the opportunity to be able to mold more students, but the time and energy to do so can be lacking. Hence, the reason I wrote this book.

I had the prompting from God to write a book long before I actually started writing. I was just looking for any way to get out of medicine, and I figured I would write a best-selling book and become a motivational speaker. This was a wild dream since I hate public speaking. It will be a complete act of God for that to happen!

I started off writing about things some black people do that annoy me. I actually wrote seven chapters. Because I wanted to be seen as a credible writer, I joined the NC Writers Network, and I went to their winter conference. I even submitted a few chapters of my writing in a critique session.

The editor and published author who read my submissions enjoyed what I wrote, but they both had similar comments. When I met with the author, she slid a copy of my submission with a plethora of notes written on it. I instantly thought, Uh oh, this may not be good.

She started off, "I thought your writing was good. I enjoyed your voice and what you wrote was interesting. But my question to you is, 'What makes this something people are going to want to read?' It's simply your opinion. If you want it to be more credible, you're going to have to approach it a different way with statistics and hard facts."

That wasn't the best news, but I still had a snippet of hope left; all the writing I did was going to lead to something. What she said next gave me even more hope.

"Something you may want to consider is writing a memoir. Then you can get away with not doing any research, and it can all be told from your point of view."

That made me smile because suddenly I knew what God wanted me to do. One of the chapters I submitted was about the young lady in the ED who was happy she was pregnant despite the fact she was just eighteen years old. Please don't judge me, but the title of the chapter was, "Is Your Child a Check?" At that time, I was not focused on uplifting people; I was just looking for an exit strategy out of medicine, so I wasn't writing the most encouraging topics. I wrote what I thought would get me attention, and drama does sell. After hearing what the author told me, I changed the focus of my writing.

The editor I met with at the conference later that afternoon gave me similar feedback, but she also mentioned how humorous she thought I was. Of course,

I liked her critique more than the author because of this. However, I was receptive to the author's comments because when the editor said I should think of other avenues of writing, I interjected.

"After listening to the author I met with this morning, I'm going to write a memoir."

She smiled back at me, "You know what? I didn't think of that, but I think you would be perfect to write a memoir."

I was overjoyed by that point, and I knew God's plan for me. I left the conference glad I attended and determined to get started along this new path.

I had various reasons for writing this memoir. First, I wanted to reach as many people like Kedeja as I could, to let them know that despite past failings, underprivileged upbringings, or seemingly insurmountable obstacles, you can succeed and do amazing things. Some will never get to meet people they want to emulate, but by just hearing their stories, they may be inspired to work harder, try harder, and actually believe greater things are in store for them.

Secondly, I wanted to be an example to show people there is not only one way to reach a desired end. If I'd listened to other people's advice regarding what I needed to do in order to get into medical school, I probably would not have made it in. If I had listened to my guidance counselor and gone to UNC Chapel Hill, I may have become lost in the shuffle of a bazillion students, and I could have flunked out. Furthermore, if I had listened to the professor who told me I would have to quit the band, I might not have developed into the leader I am today.

Third, I want to attest you don't have to let harsh situations and environments change who you are. God put us in this world to be a light. Sometimes people or events can dim that light. Don't let it stay dim. Stay prayed up and keep studying the Word of God so you don't become numb. Medicine is hard and can be frustrating. Residency was often overwhelming, and getting out to practice on my own wasn't anything like residency, but the trajectory of medicine makes it more difficult as the years go by to remain a beacon of light that provides hope for patients. Allow God to fill your heart so darkness can never enter it. Learn about the fruits of the spirit and display them daily (Galatians 5:22-23).

Finally, I want people to understand that because of my relationship with God, I have been put in the right places, and I knew the paths I should follow. I have been working on this book for almost four years now. I strategically took my time because I wanted to produce quality work that would be impactful and purposeful. I want to be considered a serious writer, and I want to leave a lasting impression on the world. Until I shared various parts of my life with co-workers, I never felt like I had a story interesting enough to make anyone want to read it. It was only after one of my nurses, Trent, told me my stories were not only interesting but uplifting that I really knew that I had a story that not only black women could relate to, but anyone with some sort of obstacle could learn from.

I hope you walk away from this knowing with God, anything is possible. Circumstances can't stop His plan as long as you follow His path. People can put limitations on themselves and others. If you do things the way people direct you, you may miss the instructions God gives you. The good thing for me is, early in life, I was stubborn and determined to do my own thing, which turned out to be God's way. I also didn't know I was at a disadvantage until I was older. Because of my exposure to different people, places, and situations, I always felt like I could be successful. There is someone reading this right now who feels like they will never amount to anything. I'm telling you right now, success only comes to those who believe they can achieve. Whatever is clouding your view, making you think you are not good enough, look past the clouds to God and let Him order your steps. Then watch God make miracles happen. He did it for me, and He can do it for you!

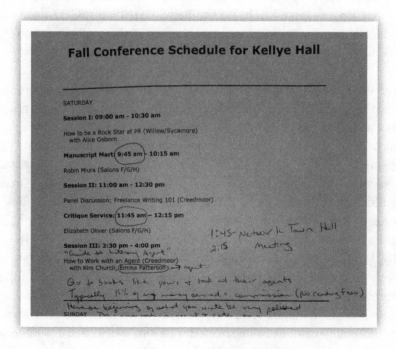

NORTH CAROLINA WRITERS' NETWORK
2016 FALL CONFERENCE SCHEDULE
Room Assignments Subject to Change

FRIDAY, NOVEMBER 4

3 – 10 pm	Registration Open	Crabtree Foyer
5 – 9 pm	Exhibits Open	Crabtree Foyer
5 – 10 pm	Book Sales Open	Magnolia
7 – 8 pm	Opening Reception *Sponsored by Alice Osborn: Editor/Book Coach/Author*	City of Oaks Ballroom
8 – 9 pm	Keynote Address by **Margaret Maron**	Crabtree Ballroom
9 – 10 pm	Margaret Maron Book Signing *Sponsored by the 2017 Piedmont Laureate Program*	Magnolia

SATURDAY, NOVEMBER 5

7:30 – 9 am	Continental Breakfast Available	Crabtree Foyer
8 am – 7:30 pm	Registration & Exhibits Open	Crabtree Foyer
8 am – 7:30 pm	Book Sales Open	Magnolia
8 – 9 am	All Stories Connect Panel Discussion: "A Conversation about Culture" with Shervon Cassim, Donna Miscolta, Elaine Neil Orr, & Sheila Smith McKoy	Crabtree Ballroom

9 – 10:30 am	Session I	
	Minute Particulars (fiction) with Kim Church	Creedmoor
	Image & Narrative (poetry) with Joseph Millar	Dogwood
	How to be a Rock Star at PR with Alice Osborn	Willow/Sycamore
	The Art of Memory: Creative Nonfiction Master Class w/ Haven Kimmel	Salon A
	The Power of Subtext: Fiction Master Class w/ Angela Davis-Gardner	Salon B
	At Work with the Masters: Poetry Master Class w/ Dorianne Laux	Salon C
	Manuscript Mart/Critique Service	Salons F/G/H

10:30 – 11 am	Break	

11 am – 12:30 pm	Session II	
	Panel Discussion: Freelance Writing 101 with *Triangle Area Freelancers*	Creedmoor
	The Contemporary Haiku with Lenard D. Moore	Dogwood
	Copyright Infringement with Mitchell Tuchman	Willow/Sycamore
	The Art of Memory: Creative Nonfiction Master Class w/ Haven Kimmel	Salon A
	The Power of Subtext: Fiction Master Class w/ Angela Davis-Gardner	Salon B
	At Work with the Masters: Poetry Master Class w/ Dorianne Laux	Salon C
	Manuscript Mart/Critique Service	Salons F/G/H

12:30 – 1:30 pm	Luncheon, with panel discussion on **Food Writing** with Bridgette A. Lacy, Debbie Moose, & **John Shelton Reed** *Sponsored by UNC Press*	Crabtree Ballroom
1:45 – 2:15 pm	Network Town Hall Meeting	Crabtree Ballroom

MOMENT OF REFLECTION

I want to take this time to help bring someone to Christ. I am not a preacher, but I am a disciple of God, and I feel it is my duty to help someone who wants to be saved and live their life for Christ. If you are not saved but want to be, say this prayer right now:

Father, in the name of Jesus, I believe that Jesus died and rose from the dead for me. You are my Lord, my savior, my healer, my protector. I know that I have sinned, but I also know that You have saved me. Come into my heart, and help me learn what it means to live for You every day. I am forever forgiven and forever saved.
Amen!

I recommend visiting websites like joycemeyer.org/salvation or josephprince. com. The churches I have attended and become members of are Koinonia Christian Center at kccfamily.com, Destiny Christian Center at leestokes.org, and Reconciling the World Ministries at rtwm.org. A wealth of resources is at your disposal, and I recommend any or all of these churches so they can pray with you and guide you.

For those who are already saved, take a moment to thank God for Jesus. Try to spread the Word to someone who doesn't know Him today!

THE COMING ATTRACTIONS

We had just finished our seasonal performance, Project: FULL OUT. Ana, the founder of our dance studio as well as the head choreographer, writer, and producer of our performance show, was moving to LA, which meant NC Dance District was closing for good. I was already mourning my short-lived dance career, and I thought I might not get to see my new dance friends anymore. I was a new member of the crew, and the studio was the thing connecting us. Therefore, I imagined it would only be a matter of time before my dance family would be splintered, and I'd be back to watching TV and playing video games on my days off.

However, the next day, I got a GroupMe message about a surprise birthday celebration for Alex, one of the choreographers for NC Dance District. The notification popping up on my phone was enough to catapult my emotions into pure joy, but at the same time, it made me sad again. I had just gotten used to the idea of not being around the gang anymore, so knowing I would be hanging out with them one last time, only to have to say goodbye again, made me second-guess whether I wanted to go. The idea of having fun and then letting them go again was heart-wrenching.

I couldn't let Alex down, though. Plus, I was off work the next couple of days, and typically when I got invited to parties at the last minute, I couldn't go because I would be scheduled for a shift. I decided to get my emotions together and enjoy the last remnants of NC Dance District out on the town.

When I arrived at the hotel with the rooftop lounge, I instantly spotted my crew seated on sofas toward the back of the venue. I immediately smiled. It was amazing how upbeat I could be just seeing my artistic bunch of friends. I went around hugging everyone who was already there, then took a seat at the edge of one of the plush outdoor couches. It was a toasty summer evening, but I was glad to be out in the heat, as opposed to being in a cold medical office. The warm breeze was a welcoming offset to the sun beaming down overhead. Because it was a surprise, Alex wasn't there yet. Ana was bringing him. I got into a conversation with choreographers Allison and Tiffany, then felt the vibration of my phone in my purse.

Ana had just notified us she and Alex were on the way up. We all got out of our seats to hide behind the bar so we could startle Alex when he arrived. It seemed like hours had passed before we actually saw Alex come around the corner.

"SURPRIIIIIISSE!" we all yelled in unison.

The look on Alex's face was worth every ounce of anxiety I had experienced deciding if I was going to show up to the party or not.

Alex screamed at the top of his lungs, "Y'all don't know how mad I was! I was in my feelings 'cause I thought nobody cared it was my birthday! I can't believe y'all!"

We all laughed as he went around hugging each of us. We then presented him with our cards and gifts and watched him view birthday messages, which we pre-recorded prior to coming, on Ana's iPad.

I was in pure bliss, seated with other dancers like myself. I looked around at the circle of new-found friends, treasuring every final moment I would have with them. Ana was seated in a chair diagonal from me, so per usual, we became engaged in conversation.

It all started off lighthearted; then as we always do, Ana and I got deep into a discussion about the future. That's what I loved about Ana. She was a dreamer like me. We both had big ideas and visions for our future lives, and we fed off each other's ambitions.

I asked, "So, what's next Ana?"

"Well, I'm thinking of taking Project: FULL OUT to other cities. I have some studios that are interested, so I'm gonna be traveling, trying to work on some details."

I could see the excitement in her eyes. I was happy for her, but honestly, I didn't want her to go. I knew she wouldn't be satisfied with Charlotte anymore; I could tell after she got back from her trip to LA. Despite the fact our bond was only about six months old, I felt her need to do and see more, and when she had informed us she wasn't renewing the lease for the studio a couple of months earlier, I knew she would soon be out of Charlotte.

As she continued talking about her new plans for success, out of nowhere, she asked, "Kellye, when are you getting out of medicine?"

Without a second thought, I sat up in my chair, leaned toward her while resting my arms on my knees, looked her straight in the eyes, and blurted out with a neck roll and a head bob, "I don't know, Ana. When am I getting out of medicine?"

That was a Nickye thought that slid out my mouth. Typically, I'm very calculated when it comes to my responses to questions. I always like to think before I speak. However, that statement was so bold and so thoughtless, it even took me by surprise.

Ana didn't miss a beat. "All I'm saying is, when I call, you better pack your bags!"

Suddenly, I was excited again. Could my dancer dreams be revived? Could Ana hold the key to me reawakening a passion I didn't realize meant so much to me? While she was talking to me, my thoughts began to race. Would I really leave medicine? What could I possibly do in Ana's world? She was a trained dancer and devoted much of her adult life to her craft. While I was a good dancer and performer, I was forty-one years old and had spent my entire young life preparing to be a doctor; for most of my adult life, I actually was a doctor.

The night went on. We had a ball eating and singing karaoke, and then it was over. As I went home and reflected on the night's events, I couldn't help but be hopeful about a change in my career path. As I tried to sleep, I kept hearing Ana's voice in my head asking, "Kellye, when are you getting out of medicine?" Did I ever tell her I was going to get out of medicine? She knew how I felt my purpose in life shifting to other things, but I didn't recall ever verbalizing I would entirely leave the practice of medicine. Where did she get that idea from?

When I finally did fall asleep, it was around three in the morning. I awoke later that day, not only physically, but spiritually. Maybe it was time to do what really made me happy. Maybe I could open a dance studio. But I had no clue how to run a dance studio. Could I really do it? Would I be brave enough to do it? Most importantly, would someone, namely Ana, help me do it?

STAY TUNED FOR MY NEXT MEMOIR:
THE DAY I WOKE UP: FROM DOCTOR TO DANCER

CITATIONS FOR SONG REFERENCES
IN CHAPTER TITLES

I Was Here. Accessed February 9, 2020. https://www.youtube.com/watch?v=i41qWJ6QjPI.

Brenda's Got A Baby. Accessed February 9, 2020. https://www.youtube.com/watch?v=NRWUs0KtB-I.

Isn't She Lovely. Accessed February 9, 2020. https://www.youtube.com/watch?v=oE56g61mW44.

Darling Nikki. Accessed February 9, 2020. https://www.youtube.com/watch?v=j8oxXkUjYHg.

Eye of the Tiger. Accessed March 30, 2020. https://www.youtube.com/watch?v=btPJPFnesV4.

I Can. Accessed March 30, 2020. https://www.youtube.com/watch?v=RvVf-gvHucRY.

Don't Stop the Music. Accessed March 30, 2020. https://www.youtube.com/watch?v=yd8jh9QYfEs.

Mercedes Boy. Accessed March 30, 2020. https://www.youtube.com/watch?v=PvganA6nrf0.

Heal the World. https://www.youtube.com/watch?v=BWf-eARnf6U. Fantasy. Accessed February 9, 2020. https://www.youtube.com/watch?v=r58GQYFZeLE.

Survivor. Accessed February 9, 2020. https://www.youtube.com/watch?v=W-mc8bQoL-J0.

The Proud. Accessed February 9, 2020. https://www.youtube.com/watch?v=HFSiM874Jxg.

Fighter. Accessed March 30, 2020. https://www.youtube.com/watch?v=P-strAfoMKIc.

Praise Him in Advance. Accessed April 4, 2020. https://www.youtube.com/watch?v=PvganA6nrf0.

Do You Know. Accessed February 9, 2020. https://www.youtube.com/watch?v=ySkca7UtnZA.

What They Gonna Do. Accessed February 9, 2020. https://www.youtube.com/watch?v=577HrFVjOPg.

One Sweet Day. https://www.youtube.com/watch?v=UXxRyNvTPr8.

God's Plan. Accessed February 9, 2020. https://www.youtube.com/watch?v=-m1a_GqJf02M.

ACKNOWLEDGEMENTS

I must start by giving all glory, honor, and praise to my Heavenly Father, who knows my beginning and my end, Jesus, the source of my salvation, and the Holy Spirit, who prompts me and guides me. Without the Holy Trinity, I am nothing.

For the physical vessels who created me, the parentals. I thank you, Mom, for being an example of a strong, independent woman. Dad, I thank you because I inherited your charm and wit. Thank you both for never allowing me to accept obstacles in life as barriers to success. Because of you two, I always felt I could accomplish anything.

On that same note, I have to thank my sisters for laughs and pure comedy. Thank you, Kim, for always being there to debate absolutely everything, and thank you, Kourt, for keeping Kim and me from erupting into fights since we don't agree on anything. I love having you two as my sisters.

Although my husband Eric didn't have a role in the development of this memoir, thank you for understanding and waiting to have a role in memoir number two!

Thanks to the rest of my family: aunts, uncles, cousins, nieces, and nephews. I can honestly say I love all of you and have had amazing experiences with you. Ft. Lauderdale, you gave me my grit. Raleigh, you gave me memories I will cherish forever.

I had some amazing teachers and principals along the way, so each of you can take some credit as well. I can gladly say, from preschool at Creative Learning Center with Ms. King up through high school, there was never one who ever doubted I would do great things, so thank you for believing in me.

I cannot forget the surrogate parents I had along the way. Pretty much all the ladies of the Oxford-Henderson Alumnae chapter of Delta Sigma Theta helped rear me. I have a lot of Omega Psi Phi fathers, other than my dad, who showed me powerful examples of good black men.

Moving along to my college crew: Thank you to every person I ever encountered in the Blue and Gold Marching Machine. I attribute a great deal of my leadership skills and development to this group of people. Dr. Hodge saw my potential when I didn't think he did. Kenny, now Dr. Ruff, I could never really read him, so that kept me on my toes. Anthony Criss gets so much credit. Watching him made me want to be him, and he molded me from an early age to the drum major I am today. This "drum major thing" is still keeping my name in people's mouths, and I'm here for it. My Tau Beta Sigma sorority sisters before and after me, keep pushing me to be great. Theta Zeta, you all are my heart! My Delta Sigma Theta sorority sisters, thank you for your support to this day.

Despite my rough time in medical school and residency, I do want to thank you all, whether you played a hero or a villain in my development. Thank you, Dr. Virginia Hardy, for putting up with me when I didn't want to put up with you. It was all me, not you! You helped me get over the test-taking hurdle. To my ED and trauma female attendings, I admired your dominance in medicine amongst all the guys. Thanks for showing me how to be seen and heard amid the men.

Thank you to those young ladies I have mentored along the way. Kedeja, you get the most kudos because your transformation is what made me want to keep doing greater things to inspire other young women. Shante, you were actually my very first mentee, so thank you for being the foundation. Lexy, Camille, Naomi, Christen, Adjoray, Kiana, Elyse, Gabby, Destiny, and Kambria, I kept trying to be the best role model I could because I want you all to be even better than me.

I have a plethora of strong women I admire, and because of your love and influence, I grew confident and more comfortable in my own skin. Your guidance made me want to mold others the way you all molded me. I think of you all as the big sisters I never had. Thank you, Amy and Toiya. You two were the best babysitters ever. Kelly Welborn, you are so outstanding. I never knew doing a cheer in the stands at A&T football games would have connected me with such a caring and kind-hearted person. Stephanie Pankey Veal, you have been a constant source of admiration. I would have to say you probably are the reason my shoe game is on point. From the first time I saw you yelling at Golden Delight, I knew I never wanted to be on your bad side, so I'm glad you had a soft spot for me.

Thank you, everyone involved at United House Publishing, especially Amber. Meeting you at Stolen Lunches Bible Study has been the best blessing ever! Thank you, Jacinda, for having her speak at Bible study, and then looking over at me when she mentioned her publishing services. You both were sent by God. Caitlyn, thank you, for editing my rough drafts. I feel like I needed to remediate English with all the strike-outs and sentence restructuring. Thank you for making me sound educated. Thank you, Miranda and Heather, for your inspirational coaching calls. Thank you, Domenica Ruta, for being my first memoir writing teacher, for giving me such constructive feedback, and for making me believe I could actually write a memoir people would want to read.

Thank you, Todgi, for my dope book cover sketch. I look like a superhero! Thank you, Trent, for the title of the book.

Finally, thank you, Kiera Vargas, for making a pact with me that we would become published authors. Your foreword is a tear-jerker. Having your constant support and motivation kept me on task to complete our mission.

I'm sure there are people I may have left out. Charge it to my head being scrambled from years of sleep deprivation and not my heart. But to any person that ever made an impression on me, good or bad, I thank you, because all of those influences made me who I am today. God bless everyone!

ABOUT THE AUTHOR

Kellye Nichelle Worth Hall is a Board-Certified Emergency Physician currently practicing in Charlotte, North Carolina. She has practiced medicine for seventeen years, thirteen of those being in the Emergency Department. She was a regular writer for the blog "LovelyeSpirit.com" where she had her own monthly segment called, "Ask the Doctor" which encouraged readers to ask questions anonymously that they may not want to ask their own physician. Additionally, she has been a contributing writer in another blog, "Women in White Coats." She is a two-time, bestselling author as a contributing writer in The HBCU Experience Anthology: North Carolina Agricultural & Technical State University Edition and an expert author in The HBCU Experience: The HBCU Band Alumni Edition.

Born in Rochester, New York, but raised in Soul City, North Carolina, she fulfilled her dream of becoming a physician by attending college at North Carolina Agricultural and Technical State University in Greensboro, North Carolina. She attended medical school at The Brody School of Medicine at East Carolina University and stayed there for her emergency medicine residency. Her experiences in the field of emergency medicine have led to her desire to write about her experiences with people, both in and out of medicine.

She is currently working in urgent care in Charlotte, North Carolina which allows her time to work on her other hobbies. Over the past three years, she has returned to her true passion, dance. While it was always God's plan for her to be a physician, in 2019, she joined forces with former NBA dancer and hip-hop dance studio owner Ana Ogbueze to become the first franchisee of NC Dance District, Incorporated, Charlotte location. She is a dancer with Project: FULL OUT, an NC Dance District affiliate, as well as with The Dance District Agency. She is married to her husband Eric Hall, and she has three fur babies, her dogs, Mumslye, Kooler, and Germonye.

Facebook Handle:	Kellye Worth Hall
Instagram:	kellyedont4get_the_e
Twitter:	AggieDivaDoc
Websites:	www.drkellyewhall.com
	www.ncdancedistrict.com

9 781952 840081